Ildiko SpinFisher is a biofield psychologist and the Founder of Life Retuning. She has run a successful global practice since 2004, working with over 1000 clients and helping them both personally and within their businesses and careers. She specialises in working with entrepreneurs as a Business Empowerment Facilitator and runs regular courses teaching her Life Retuning system.

Ildiko is qualified in several alternative health and wellness modalities, including NLP, aromatherapy and hypnotherapy. She is passionate about teaching energy-based living and healthy energy-awareness in our ever-increasing technological world. She has been featured in several publications, has been the guest of numerous interviewers and was the UK Editor of a global online magazine. Discover more at her website: www.liferetuning.com.

ENERGY AWARE

Live a Life of No Mistakes

Ildiko SpinFisher

To Craig,
wishing you abundant joy
and success

warm wishes
Ildikó

20.05.21

FLYING
SQUAD

Energy Aware

ISBN 978-1-914209-04-8

eISBN 978-1-914209-05-5

Published in 2021 by Flying Squad Books

© Ildiko SpinFisher 2021

Mandala on page 180 used by kind permission of Pixabay: https://pixabay.com/service/license/

Contents

To all of humanity and for the future.

Interactive QR Code and Link

A couple of the exercises in this book invite you to work with resources found on my website. You can access these resources by scanning the following QR tag with the camera on your smartphone or tablet:

Alternatively, you can access them by following this link: https://www.liferetuning.com/energy-aware-interactive/

Introduction

I wrote this book because I felt compelled to share some very good news with you. There is a gift waiting for you to open. There is a huge part of your birthright as a human being that you are probably unaware of. I discovered it gradually through several years of searching for an answer to my own problems. But when I found the answer, it blew my mind.

I learnt that the way our world really functions is very different to what we have been told. There is a hidden domain which is the vibrational database of all life. It is the most powerful, invisible force you didn't realise you had. But when you start using it, you will find that it will become indispensable. It will super-charge your life and give you the ability to end patterns of making recurring mistakes. No more unfulfilling partners, no more jobs that undervalue you, no more fair-weather friends, no more disappointing outcomes. Knowing about this database will change the way you make choices forever!

In order for you to understand the enormity of what I will be sharing in *Energy Aware*, I am going to tell you the story of the journey that led to my discovery.

Have you ever scooped up a handful of sand and watched it trickling away through your fingers? Imagine if you were unable to stop the trickle but just looked on helplessly as it gradually disappeared. When I was 24 years old, that is how my life felt. It started with short-term memory loss – whole days just became a blank. I had a busy life in London; I worked hard, went out a lot and my brain was always buzzing. So I didn't think too much about the blanks.

But the big shock came one day when I was travelling on the Tube in the summer. I was rammed in the middle of a group of sweaty tourists. Suddenly the train stopped in the tunnel and the lights went off. There was no announcement. We just stood there in the stifling heat and dark, not knowing how long it would be before we could escape into the fresh air. I felt my throat tighten with a sharp pang of fear. My mind told me that I couldn't breathe and that the oxygen would run out. I had my first ever panic attack; gasping for air and desperate to get out. I visualised myself screaming and beating down the doors. I felt like a trapped animal who was going to die.

In that moment, I didn't realise that my life as I had known it was going to change forever. That I would descend into the worst hell and then rise into an extraordinary life, beyond my wildest dreams of how good things could be. But on that day my mind became my jailer. It was as if I had been fitted with a restrictive collar that caused pain and fear whenever I tried to push beyond the invisible barriers of a very narrow arena of activities. It came as a huge shock, but now I know that it was highly predictable because of the ways I chose to live my life. My consciousness had forced me to the end of the line and it was time to wake up to what was really going on.

Day after day, I could only concentrate on how I was going to survive the next hour without having a panic attack. I had good cause to dread it: I started having several attacks a day. Each time I had a panic attack I thought I was going to suffocate and die. For me, there was only one acceptable way to go from this place and that was up and out. I spent the next seven years looking for the exit without finding it. Nothing I tried helped me to recover – and then the wheel of fortune turned, I walked through a portal and a veil was lifted from my eyes.

On the other side, I found the way to completely deconstruct the old me. I freed myself up from my destructive thought patterns and emotional baggage. I discovered how to reconstruct myself and design my life the way I wanted it to be.

So I am speaking to you from the future, your future. I am standing calling to you from the other side of the bridge. I am telling you that there is a way across the divide, a way out of recurring disappointment with relationships, the jadedness of worn-out jobs and the inevitability of unhappy outcomes. There is a famous scene in the film *Indiana Jones and the Last Crusade*, where Indiana is faced with a yawning chasm. He throws a handful of sand out ahead of him and it reveals a hidden path across the gorge. That is what I am going to share with you in *Energy Aware*: the hidden route map that exists within you and around you. You will be able to throw your own handful of sand and walk the path ahead to your own empowerment.

During my journey to find the way out of my own pain, I did a lot of training. I qualified as a clinical and holistic aromatherapist, a hypnotherapist, NLP practitioner and a life coach. I gained qualifications in Indian champissage, reiki, energy psychology, anatomy and physiology, and reflexology massage. None of those modalities helped me significantly on a personal level, but I gained a vast amount of knowledge about an alternative way of seeing the world. I built up a portfolio of satisfied clients who loved me using these modalities, so I could see how effective they were.

But I still needed to understand the hidden, tiny world that seemed to be telling a very different story about how our bodies function and the world at large works. I decided to study quantum physics and the portal opened before me. Gradually a fantastic tale of ancient energy revealed itself. A binding of living cells with distant stars, invisible pathways and patterns; a whole different world. A tale of the fundamental vibrations that we are made of. A deep mirroring of what the ancient civilisations and indigenous people had known and still know the truth of.

I now understood how to bring quantumness into psychology and started using it on myself. I became my own vibrational laboratory. By reading the energetic patterns of the emotional baggage and self-limiting perceptions I had been carrying for years, I was able to reverse those patterns and free myself from the restrictions on my life that I had been trapped in. I discovered the way to unlock my own prison door, step outside and become a person who happens *to* life instead of one whom life happens to.

I have become empowered in everything I do. The choices I make now are underpinned with a solid understanding of the reality of a situation and how to obtain the best desired outcome. I turned my breakdown into my breakthrough and I am blessed to live an extraordinary life. *Energy Aware* reveals the path for you to get there too.

I started using what I had discovered and developed with my clients. The levels of success blew me away. Decades of emotional and mental pain started rapidly dissolving through working on altering the energy of people, without the need to discuss anything. I developed a system that I call Life Retuning, and I have now been running my Life Retuning practice for many years. The level of success is consistent for my clients, no matter what issue we work together on. It is all down to energy.

Today, I work with clients all over the globe and I witness how hidden pathways connect us in extraordinary ways – and that is all down to energy too. You will discover by reading *Energy Aware* what energy actually is at a fundamental level. You will find out why knowing about the quantum world is vital for your wellbeing.

How to Use this Book

This is not a book about how to use your mind to improve your life. Instead, *Energy Aware* introduces you to the vast ocean of vibrational information that lies beyond logic. The natural world has been using it successfully for billions of years. Your mind is only a small part of it. Our intellect-dominated world has shunned this invisible resource for many centuries as being irrelevant to living a fulfilled life. Yet not being aware of it is like wearing a blindfold and aiming to hit a target without knowing which direction you are facing. No wonder the choices you make can often fall short of the fulfilment and joy you yearn for. Imagine if you could rip off the blindfold and hit a bullseye every time? *Energy Aware* introduces you to a revolutionary new way of living. It reveals that hidden domain which is the vibrational database of all life. Your greater consciousness and energetic awareness permeate every part of it.

There are 24 Energy Aware Principles at the core of this radical new approach. They offer daily touchstones that are the key to forming deeper relationships, attaining higher levels of contentment and being able to accomplish the extraordinary. Each Principle combines a profound insight into our human motivations and reactions, with a clear view into the energetic patterns and sign posts that are always present. This gives you a ground-breaking advantage in making your choices consistently successful.

The 24 Energy Aware Principles are arranged into three parts: those relating to personal energy, to relationship energy and to global energy. They reveal how you are in constant relationship with everyone and everything. They clarify how you can go beyond your thoughts and use the currents of vibrational information as a force for good, which will catapult you into living your life at a higher pitch.

At the back of the book, you will find the Energy Aware quick reference table: this is a go-to place where you can find the guidance you need to get out of negative emotions and states of mind. It provides a clarification of what is happening for you both psychologically and energetically. A set of specifically designed Energy Aware tools then provide the solution for how to get back on track and maximise your potential.

If you have had enough of disappointments and are hungry for a radically different approach to solving your problems, then this book is for you. It will show you how you can harness energy and super-charge your life. Within the pages of *Energy Aware*, you will find out how to be in charge of your own destiny. You will discover how to do things right and have a meaningful impact, both as an inner activist and an outer change maker.

This book is designed to fit in with your life as an easy companion. But like any companion, you will need to get to know it first, so I suggest that you read it through from cover to cover and then use it as a practical guide throughout your day-to-day life. If you are feeling confused, unhappy or restless – especially if you need to make a decision – go straight to the Energy Aware quick reference table on page 203. Follow the steps to bring yourself into a place of clarity and certainty.

Let *Energy Aware* be your guiding light to help you navigate your life in a radically new way. You are going to discover how to unlock the power of energy and use it to transform your life, your relationships and the world you live in.

The Wise Child Inside You

Your personal energy might have seemed a strange concept to you in the past. Maybe you have read books about the chakras, the aura or extrasensory perception. Perhaps you've sat through talks by healers and therapists, or attended workshops where you discovered something out of the ordinary, which made you think. But as for energy being a part of your day-to-day world – perhaps you have not yet considered that every breath you take, every thought you have and all your actions could be governed by an all-pervading electrical field?

This way of seeing the world and experiencing life is a radically new way of approaching things. It involves taking one of those giant leaps in conscious awareness that is so significant it is life-altering. Like when people went from thinking the Earth was flat to suddenly finding out that it is actually a sphere, or assuming that we are the only inhabited planet and then seeing an alien for the first time. It's a head-twister! It changes everything and nothing will ever be the same again. I know, because I have been through this total shake-up and it took me from living an ordinary life, where I struggled with understanding myself, to stepping into an extraordinary, redesigned life with energy in the driving seat.

If we are really honest with ourselves, we can look back over the years and see the seeds of the main themes of our lives, before they germinate and start growing into our achievements. For example, when I was a child, I didn't spend my time with dollies or My Little Pony toys. Instead, I was fascinated by the strange things around me. I found that if I stared at a white pattern on a black background for a few seconds, when I looked at a plain white sheet immediately afterwards, I would see the negative of the pattern appear on the paper. My eyes were acting like some kind of internal projector. I noticed repeating patterns everywhere in nature. I would get totally absorbed in looking at the distorted reflections of the sun on water or light through a bottle. I sketched a lot and often lost myself in trying to capture these fragmented patterns in pastels and paint.

Today, I still see and interpret the world in patterns, and this enables me to notice what is true as opposed to what I am told is true. We all fix our way of interacting with the world at a young age, but few of us are left to develop it without being corrected by the well-meaning adults around us. We start to deviate from our inner knowing and instead are taught to listen to our minds. We are told that we must do things in a certain way, because it has always been done like that. Often, our real instincts become diluted as we are taught to relate to ourselves and the world in ways that are based on what others want us to know. Eventually we fall into a new pattern, one dominated by logic and what our eyes can perceive.

But it is striking how we accept the world just as it is when we are children. Do you remember finding out something odd and exciting – and then being told by the adults that it wasn't possible? Many people can recall regularly talking to an invisible friend, or even seeing a fully solid person, and then have Mum or Dad tell them they were making it up. Maybe you had a little routine, a secret, magical way of communing with the world that you thought only you knew about – until much later on.

I have often found that I naturally did things as a child, which later in life I discovered a professor or specialist had written a prestigious book about. Or I did something just because it felt good, which turned out to be a form of ancient practice performed by sages of old. This happened, for example, with the way I used to sit, quieten my mind and focus on one single point for a long time. Years later, I went to a meditation class and as the orange-clad yogi sat cross-legged and started explaining how to reach that point of stillness, I was surprised. What he was describing was what I had done so naturally as a child. I had no idea until then that other people did it and that it was called meditation!

Exploring Beyond the Edge

Sometimes childhood curiosity and investigating the truth might come close to getting us into real hot water! When I was still at primary school, I discovered an incredible, exciting and potentially risky phenomenon. Risky because I went to a Catholic school. At the end of the day, my mum would drive to school to collect me and she would pick up a couple of my school friends at the same time. As their mums were working, they would stay at our house for a few hours until they could be collected by their parents.

While they waited at our house, sometimes we would play an intriguing game. We would place five objects in front of us: a pair of sunglasses, a pebble, an elastic band, a toy car and a paperclip, for example. Then we took turns to choose an object to focus on. We would write down our choice, hide it from each other and try to send a mental message to the other person, willing them to pick up on what we had chosen to focus on. I would imagine the back of my friend's head and send an image of the object into it. It was simple. I soon learnt that the scores for correct answers were really high with some friends, whereas it didn't seem to work with others. I had no idea why that was. It was only much later that I read about telepathy and realised to all intents and purposes, I had managed to devise a scientific experiment into extrasensory perception! I was ten years old at the time.

I didn't have a clue about why our game worked; I just accepted that it did. I didn't ask anybody to explain and, as I went to a school run by nuns, I couldn't ask any questions about what I was experimenting with. In a place where we had to say a Latin prayer at the beginning of each class, I could never have talked about being able to read other people's projected thoughts. I was once severely told off just for daring to ask an allegedly blasphemous question. I wanted to know where the evidence was for the 14 Stations of the Cross. My religious studies teacher fixed me with a baleful eye and told me in no uncertain terms that I must have blind faith and I had no right to question the divine. I got the feeling she was scanning me for a tail and hooves. If she had known what I was experimenting with, I'm sure I would have been scheduled for an exorcism!

Like me, you might have experimented as a child with things that fascinated you. Maybe you wondered why you sometimes got a nasty electric shock when you touched the family car; or why if you vigorously combed your hair upside down, it bushed out and when you pulled your fingers through it, it crackled and stuck to your hand. What you were encountering was your own personal energy.

When you hear about chakras and channelling and other seemingly unexplainable things, these really aren't as strange as they might appear to be. It is just that modern science has not yet developed the equipment to substantiate much of this bio-energetic phenomena. The research that has been done is not mainstream and was hard won by researchers, who for many years had to battle against derision and being ostracised by their scientific colleagues. Moreover, ancient practices are often not taken seriously by our mind-driven society. So, you see, we need to get all of that prejudice out of the way before we can find out what is really going on.

A great place to start is with the tangible energy that allows your body to function. Have you ever wondered how your muscles work, or how you have thoughts? There are tiny and constant electrical sparks that activate and animate you. The cells in your body are all capable of using electricity. Your cell membranes function through the charged ions that create a current of electrical energy. When you feel hot, you are generating thermal energy. It is impossible to deny these simple facts – and it is these facts that start the journey into the unseen land of your energetic heritage and birthright. For electricity and heat are just two physical forms of energy. But there are other ways that energy manifests; it is an ever-changing, vibrational sea of currents and we are forever swimming within it.

So let's step over the threshold into the extraordinary world of personal electromagnetic fields. Nature is a good place to start, because animals simply accept how they live and don't question why they do what they do. They don't have to deal with fake news or social media 'likes'. They don't worry about careers or material wealth. They truthfully show us how the world works and, if we are humble enough, they can address a lot of the doubt and questions we have about our own lives.

Luminous Communication, Natural Batteries and Heightened Awareness

Light is a form of energy that we use and know well. If it wasn't for light, we would not be able to observe the world we live in. Our eyes would not be able to see the beautiful golden sunsets, the vivid blue swells of the ocean, the green leaves on the trees. But some animals have a remarkable control over light and they use it to survive. It is quite extraordinary what a complex spectrum of signalling exists around us. From fireflies to deep-sea fish to ocean turtles, light is the code of communication for mating, hunting and defence. Many animals actually create light within the cells of their bodies. A special compound called luciferin reacts with oxygen and gives them the ability to flash signals whenever they want. It is the natural kingdom's equivalent to texting!

There is another form of energy that some animals use, which is instantaneously deadly for their unfortunate prey – and that is electricity. Have you ever looked at the transmission towers with their high voltage cables running in the sky above you? If you stand still and listen, you may hear a crackle or a soft humming as the energy courses through those black lines. It is for good reason that you are likely to find a 'Danger of Death' notice on the pylon: you would not survive an electric shock. The voltage passing through those cables is 345,000 volts, a very powerful force of electricity.

In the natural world, the electric torpedo ray is one of the most dangerous sea animals on Earth. A disk-shaped, flat fish with a tail, the torpedo ray has two organs on its head that are capable of producing an electric shock of 240 volts of electricity. It wraps its disk around a fish and stuns it with an electrical storm of several rapid shocks. The electricity creates muscle spasms and the captured fish has no chance of escape. If a human were to receive a shock from an adult ray, it could knock them unconscious.

Rays are just one type of fish that uses electricity; there are over 300 others that are known about at present. How they create this form of energy shows that nature has adapted to harness the natural forces on our planet. These animals have evolved stacked cells, which form batteries – similar to the AA ones you put into your twinkly Christmas lights. They can control signals from their brains to activate those bio-batteries when they want to use the electrical charge. The force field created can stretch up to several metres out from their bodies. When swimming within an electrical field, it is possible to pick up a huge amount of information about their surroundings. Fish that use electricity in this way can detect the size, shape, speed and position of distant objects and other fish. They can even instantly tell whether another animal is dead or alive through its electrical signature.

The great white shark is a distant cousin of the torpedo ray and it is the most efficient hunter of the sea. What makes it so successful? It uses some very effective senses. The shark uses soundwaves and its internal ears are tuned to low frequencies of between 10 and 800 Hz, which is lower than a human can hear by about 10 Hz. Tiny hairs along its body can translate sound vibrations into information, helping it to find its prey even in low light. But the superior sense the shark has is electroreception. Tiny receptors called ampullae of Lorenzini on its snout pick up the electrical impulses from living organisms. This allows the shark to know even if a fish is hiding from it on the ocean floor. Like a mobile X-ray machine, the shark is constantly aware of everything in its environment as it cruises along.

At the opposite end of the animal kingdom, another creature has developed the art of sound communication to a superlative level. Spiders come in all shapes and sizes – and the tiny peacock jumping spider could sit on your thumb with plenty of room around it. These Australian spiders are called peacocks because the males are spectacularly coloured, in the most vivid patterns. These tiny, living jewels are able to distinguish colours, which is unusual for spiders – but what is also remarkable is that they use complex individual drumming sequences while dancing for a female. Just like a rap artist, they create a beat with their bodies.

Many animals use sound as a method of communication and as humans we are no different. Ancient pictograms have been found to represent individual sounds which, when put together, form a word and meaning. Sound is the vibration of pressure waves that are picked up by the eardrum inside our ears and by our bodies. If workmen are drilling outside of your house, you don't just hear the noise of the drill – you can feel it resonating through the ground and therefore through your body.

Energy exists all around us – from the oceans, to the air, to the soil beneath our feet. Have you ever sat in the garden or a meadow and watched the bees zipping backwards and forwards from one cluster of flowers to another? Have you noticed how they sometimes avoid certain flowers? I have often wondered why they do that. Well, we don't have to ponder the question anymore. The answer involves the electrical charge of energy. It turns out that bees and plants have evolved a symbiotic existence whereby both gain what they need from their relationship – and that they use energy as an important part of their exchange.

Bees are known as pollinators because they carry pollen from a male plant to a female plant, thereby ensuring that fruits grow and the plants can reproduce. A bee has hairs on its body that brush the pollen grains from a flower when it lands to collect nectar. Do you remember the static that builds up when you rub a balloon vigorously against your T-shirt so that you can stick it to yourself? When a bee flies, it develops a similar positive charge of static energy as the air rubs against its body. In contrast, a flower is part of a plant that has its roots in the soil; the Earth acts like the third prong on a plug and the flower therefore carries a negative charge. As negative attracts positive, so the bee is attracted to the flower – just like the pull of a magnet. As it lands on the flower, the positively bee-charged pollen is magnetised to the female stigma or reproductive part of the flower. So the relationship between the bee and the flower is electrical. When a bee approaches a flower, the plant calls to it energetically by pulsing a tiny negative current.

Every animal, large or small, exists with energy as a vital part of their lives. Light and electricity are two forms of natural energy and as a human you have evolved to use them – but your abilities go way beyond that.

Waking Up to Your Energy

Can you imagine going through life with one arm tied behind your back? Unhappily, I found out what that is like. I shattered my left wrist a couple of years ago. At the hospital, the surgeon told me that I had a high-impact compound fracture. Apparently, it is the number 1 injury that skateboarders suffer. I wasn't doing anything so cool as skateboarding; I just slipped down a slope. For the next two months, I had my whole arm in a cast and had to rely on doing everything with my right hand. The one thing I do with my left hand is write. So I was stuck when I was working with my clients. In the end, I had to teach myself to write with my right hand.

The lowest point came when I was trying to cut a tomato on a chopping board. My cast prevented me from being able to steady it with my left hand, so I had to kneel on the floor in the middle of my kitchen, in order to get the right angle to slice it. Then, when it came tying my rubbish bags up, I had no other option except to do it with my right hand and my teeth!

When I finally had my cast cut off, I was ecstatic! I was overjoyed at being able to use both my arms and hands again. Immediately life became so much easier. The problems I had to put up with disappeared. It was a powerful lesson, which showed me how diminished we can be when we are not using all of our natural resources.

I invite you to stretch your imagination to consider a fantastical scenario. Let's go back to our great white shark and imagine that it is able to read! It has come across a disparaging opinion which states that only 'woo-woo' sharks believe in electrical fields, as these are just pseudoscience. What would happen if it bought into this story and suddenly started doubting its incredible electroreception? This may seem like crazy thinking, but I am holding up a mirror to what happens in our human world. Not being aware of, dismissing or not using your own personal energy is like going through life using only one arm.

Mind Traps and Bright Choices

I n this book, I would like us to explore the fabric of life itself. Let's start close to home...

Have you ever had a good look at what your jeans are made of? Look closely and you will see a pattern appearing. If you hold your finger under the fabric and pull it apart a little, you will see tiny white lines showing through the blue. Those lines are revealing to you that your jeans are made of woven fabric which has then been dyed.

Weaving is an ancient skill dating back many centuries. I spent a couple of years at university studying woven textiles and got to know the weaving process intimately. For days on end, I could be found sitting inside a huge loom with a little hooked instrument called a fish, pulling thousands of threads through tiny eyelets. Those eyelets are called heddles and they are responsible for lifting the threads during the weaving process, which then form the beautiful patterns in fabric that we see. I learnt to appreciate how important each of those thousands of threads is in making up the whole. Whenever I finished threading up my loom and actually started weaving, I was always awestruck and delighted as I gradually saw the pattern of the cloth begin to appear each time I pushed the shuttle across the warp threads.

The principle of weaving is basic: the vertical threads are called the warp, through which you pass horizontal threads called the weft – and gradually you get a solid piece of cloth. While the denim fabric of your jeans is likely to be very plain, it is possible to weave complex patterns and designs into cloth. It all depends on what path the horizontal threads take through the vertical ones. Each time a choice is made, the horizontal thread is locked in as the vertical threads crossover – and a new configuration is ready for the next thread. Each new thread builds up a pattern so that when you finally look at the fabric, it all becomes clear.

Your life is like a piece of cloth and every choice you make is building up a pattern. Each time you think, act or react, your choice is locked in – just like those horizontal threads in the fabric. Just like that horizontal thread, each of your thoughts, acts and reactions determines what is or is not possible for you to create from that point onwards. Each weft thread creates a new line in the unfolding story and each choice you make adds the next line in your own story.

In weaving, it is possible to start a new pattern by changing the configuration of the way the warp threads are lifted and even the colour of the thread you use. The result will be a completely different-looking fabric. In fact, it is astonishing how different the cloth will turn out. Before weaving several metres of a particular fabric, I would create a sample cloth so that I could decide which pattern and colour palette looked the best. Depending on how I threaded up my loom, I could easily weave 30 different little squares of fabric – and each one would look totally different. Different colours and patterns showed up as I built up the weft threads.

It is the same with your choices. You can completely change the story of your life at any moment that you decide you want a different pattern.

Why Do We Make Mistakes?

Have you ever found yourself doing the following? You are faced with a decision and you recognise that you have been here before. You have had to make a similar decision in the past and it ended up making you stressed or unhappy. You vow that this time it will be different. This time you will make the right choice for you.

Then, to your horror, you find that you have made the same mistake again and everything is working out just like before. In fact, if you think about it, this is a recurring pattern of your life. It is awful, isn't it, to realise that you actually have no idea how to stop it from happening again?

MISTAKES ARE COSTLY IN
TIME + MONEY + LIFE ENERGY

There are different ways of making a choice. First, you can write down a list of pros and cons, add them up and go with the choice that seems to be the least negative and most positive. Another way is to read up on as much information as possible and then make an informed choice based on other people's opinions and experiences. Alternatively, you might make a choice based simply on whether you like the sound of something or not; or you might listen to your mind's judgements and assumptions and let the Survival Calculation guide you. (I will be explaining what that is later on in this chapter.) Or you could make a choice based on your family's traditions or values. You could just go with what you desire most, or what you think you need, without worrying about any consequences at all.

I have described the way that the majority of people make choices and have done for centuries. All these methods risk leading to a disappointing outcome, because they all fail to draw on the full spectrum of information available to make sure that the choice has the greatest chance of being the right one for the right person in the right circumstances at the right time. All of these methods could be radically improved if they were used as just one source of information, just as a means for cross-referencing options during the whole process of making a choice.

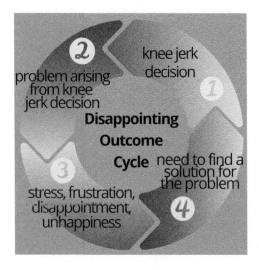

The disappointing outcome cycle

The reason you end up with the same disappointing outcome is that even though you think you have thought about and chosen your intended course of action differently this time, nothing has fundamentally changed in your underlying beliefs and perceptions.

Research shows that we usually make a decision based on our emotional response before our mind validates it as a logical choice. That emotional decision happens in a split second and we are unaware of what is really happening. Your mind might tell you a story about why you made the choice, but it is not the real reason. Your mind's story is called an 'intellectual alibi'. For example, when you buy something that is a luxury, you buy it because you want it – while your mind tells you *why* you need it.

How to recognise an intellectual alibi

If you find yourself saying any of the following, your mind is telling you a story and you are often not aware of the real reason you are about to make a choice:

➤ It worked for... someone else who has a different set of circumstances/attitude/reason/passion/resources, etc.

➤ It didn't work for someone else and therefore I'm not risking it.

➤ It is the easy, no-hassle option.

➤ If I don't act now, I will lose the opportunity.

➤ It will make me feel better/more confident/ more attractive, etc.

➤ Everyone else is doing it.

➤ I'll do it to cheer myself up.

➤ If I do this it will be the solution to my problems.
(This often applies to massive life decisions such as getting married, getting divorced, having a baby, leaving a job, taking a job.)

➤ I don't have the time.

➤ I'm not qualified enough.

➤ I'm not good with people/sums/technology/responsibility, etc.

You don't think the way you think you think!

In this chapter, I'm going to slow down the decision-making process for you so that you can start to understand what is really happening in those split seconds before you make a choice – and why you keep having disappointing outcomes.

First, let's watch the mind in action. Everywhere we look, the message is that people who can think rationally, aka 'successfully', are prized beyond measure. Those people who are cold, logical strategists have been the ones in the top positions in business, the richest individuals and the ones in power. Their minds seem to operate on an emotionless plateau of planning, goal-setting and personal achievements. They understand words such as winning, competition and ambition. We even have the saying 'it's just business' for when the most ruthless decisions are taken. There seems to be no room for emotion, and compassion, caring and empathy are labelled as 'soft skills'.

It is only fairly recently that emotional quotient, as it is termed, has been regarded as being relevant to the important aspects of life at all. The term has only been around since the 1990s, coined by two researchers called Peter Salavoy and John Mayer, who described EQ as 'a form of social intelligence that involves the ability to monitor one's own and others' feelings and emotions, to discriminate among them, and to use this information to guide one's thinking and action'. Notice how a particular type of thinking is the important end result.

The Survival Calculation

Imagine being a caveman or cavewoman. Your life would be very close to the animals. You would know what their alarm calls sound like when a predator is stalking nearby. Life would be raw, violent and, probably, short. It would be a case of kill or be killed most of the time. What sort of mind would you need? One that is constantly on the lookout for danger and opportunities.

Let's come back to the present time. You are the descendant of those cave dwellers from so long ago and you share the same fast, reactive mind. In fact, you've brought that caveman or cavewoman with you, and they are still living in your mind! Nowadays, it is much less likely that you will be faced with a kill-or-be-killed situation; our modern world has managed to reduce the possibility in so many ways. But you nevertheless inherited the 'Survival Calculation' and your mind still processes your experiences and your environment in the same way that our prehistoric ancestors did.

So what is the Survival Calculation? Your mind makes a decision about whether something happening now or in the perceived future is a threat to your physical survival. It uses the information from your past experiences to make that decision. Because this calculation takes place at the do-or-die level, your mind sees things in black and white: something is either a danger or it isn't. However, nowadays many things are much less dangerous than a full-on threat to our survival. An upsetting phone call is not likely to kill us!

The problem is that your mind does not understand emotions. Your mind's job does not include emotional understanding; a very different part of your consciousness deals with that. But your mind certainly knows how to use them! If it has flagged your situation as harmful, you are going to feel fear, anxiety, anger, frustration or a plethora of other uncomfortable emotions. We might term these responses as being negative, but actually your mind is using them to protect you. If you are frightened and you run away, your mind has done its basic job: you remove yourself from danger and you survive. Fear is such an emotionally and physically painful feeling that you have to act on it. You sweat and shiver and your breathing is short and fast. Your senses become heightened and you can't sit still. All you want is to find a way to stop this feeling, to escape from it.

Similarly, if you are angry about a situation that threatens your peace and personal space, you want to change the situation; you have the urge to fight it. You feel restless, obsessed and irrational, and you want to act no matter what. In ancient times, some of the Norse warriors going into battle would become berserkers. A red rage would descend on them, turning them into indiscriminate killing machines.

Isn't the mind an incredibly efficient emotional slave driver? It is not interested in peace, just your survival – and it will get your physical body to do anything that ensures that. If you live from your mind, your dominant impulses are likely to be reactions to danger:

Data:		Calculation:		Result:
PAST		PRESENT		WHAT YOU EXPERIENCE
Your mind takes the data of all your previous experiences that resemble the current situation.		Basic data of past experiences will trigger your mind to decide if a current or future situation is harmful or harmless… If harmful…		Emotional, mental or physical distress. Your mind's way of stopping you from either continuing in or going into a situation.
	➤		➤	YOUR MIND'S JOB IS DONE… YOU SURVIVED

The Survival Calculation:
Your experiences of events in the past = the threat levels of current + future events

29

Three Mind Traps

Now that you understand how your mind works, let's go back to how we make choices. I am going to share with you three mind traps that can send you down a blind alley to a disappointing outcome.

Knee-jerk decisions

When we make an instantaneous decision without being consciously aware of all of our unconscious triggers, we can end up creating a problem for ourselves. Knee-jerk decisions come from one of two emotional drivers: desire or fear. A decision to have something in a split second has nothing to do with a realistic assessment of the current circumstances. Knee-jerk decisions are the ones that can end up putting us in debt, difficulties and filling us with regret.

In marketing terms, we might be classed as panic buyers – as amply demonstrated by the sales of the vast amount of rolls of toilet paper that outstripped supply at the beginning of the 2020 pandemic. The term marketeers use for this kind of buying is 'impulse purchases'. This is why stores put small, affordably priced items like sweets, snacks and novelty items near the checkout, so that we will impulsively put them in our baskets while we are waiting in the line to pay: retailers know that we are likely to make an unplanned and unconscious purchase in this situation. You're giving money away for something you often do not need but you saw it and you want it. You acted on desire. There are even people who will impulse-buy a car, because the manufacturer engaged their desire, and who then regret their knee-jerk decision in the cold light of day.

Listening only to your mind and not trusting yourself

Do you trust yourself to make a good choice? I invite you to sit for a moment and cast your mind back to how many times you have made an important decision and got it right. And now think about the times when you feel you got it wrong. Can you identify what the main difference was? Often, the difference is whether you trusted yourself or not.

Making decisions carries a power with it that shapes the outcome. If you are filled with doubt from the outset as to whether you are capable of making a good decision, then you are likely to focus on your doubt rather than on other factors and any information that you are given about the situation. That narrows down the likelihood of getting it right.

If you find it hard to trust yourself to make good decisions, now is a good time to discover why that is. Maybe somebody in your family undermined your confidence in yourself when you were little? Perhaps you weren't allowed to make your own decisions when you were a child, because one of your parents always made the decisions for you? When this happens, we don't have the opportunity to develop confidence in making our own decisions – which then carries through into our adult lives. Or maybe you remember a disastrous decision that created a lot of pain for you and others at some time in your life? The fear of creating the same level of pain again may be what is stopping you from being confident in taking decisions now. It is important to understand that making good decisions is not just down to looking at the information that you have available to you. It is often the appropriateness of the timing when you take the decision that is important. Perfect timing comes down to many factors but it's possible to simplify the whole process to your advantage.

Following other people's advice without checking whether it is right for you

'It's vital to remember who you really are. It's very important. It isn't a good idea to rely on other people or things to do that for you, you see. They always get it wrong.'
– Terry Pratchett, *Sourcery*

Let's look at what actually happens when you ask someone else for their opinion about your plan. The plain fact is that most people are not good at listening. They might hear what you are saying, but that does not mean that they are listening to you. In the same way, it is possible to hear a webinar and not remember anything afterwards. However, when you listen to what is being said, this starts a process of awareness and internal response.

Why is it such a challenge to listen? Because most people are enslaved by the constant internal chatter that is the common state of the human mind. Real listening is often blocked out by buzzing thoughts about what they need to do themselves, what they have done, what other people think about them, or whether they should be doing something else. That doesn't leave much room in which to hold their mind's attention for very long, and to be sure that they are in the best place to offer you a valid opinion.

Next time you see people talking, notice whether there is an actual conversation occurring, or whether it is just two people talking at each other. Often, they are in their own separate worlds of thought. In general, we are not very good at giving each other the time and space for expressing ourselves. So you can see why relying on someone else's absolute attention to get their opinion is often not a reliable choice when it comes to making an informed choice of your own.

The Fear Mirror

Not only do we have a general tendency not to listen to what others are actually saying, there is something else that often happens when you ask someone their opinion about what you should decide to do. As you know, a person with a phobia will be specifically terrified of what triggers their fear, like heights for example, and that fear is often highly debilitating. However, when it comes to understanding someone else's phobia about spiders, for instance, this is not what they fear and they therefore cannot comprehend why spiders should be scary. In other words, we can only interpret someone else's situation based on what we have personally experienced and how we react. We cannot have any reactions to that experience other than our own; and the fact is that when you ask someone else to validate your plan or idea, they will react to it as if they were considering how that experience would be for them. If the prospect fills them with fear or doubt, they may tell you it's a bad or risky plan.

It is therefore often not reliable to ask others to validate our ideas and plans. So if we can't rely on others, then we have to rely on ourselves instead. Now that you know the traps that your mind can drop you into, it is time to find out how it can limit your options for making beneficial decisions. My aim is to make you aware of when your mind puts on the brakes.

Your Ceiling of Expectation

'[I]t is well known that a vital ingredient of success is not knowing that what you're attempting can't be done. A person ignorant of failure can be a halfbrick in the bicycle of history.'
– Terry Pratchett, *Equal Rights*

When we choose to avoid an opportunity and miss out on a chance to gain something we have been working towards, either consciously or unconsciously, it can be the result of a hidden factor. That hidden factor arises because we hit an invisible ceiling of expectation. Have you ever found yourself just within reach of a goal you've wanted to achieve for a long time and you're so close to it that you can almost taste it? Then, to your great shock, have you done something to sabotage yourself and missed out on what you wanted so much? This is because you hit a ceiling of expectation that was invisible to you.

You have set these limits in all areas of your life. They dictate how much love, abundance, health, wealth and happiness you will allow yourself to enjoy. Equally, they determine how much pain, exploitation, neglect and unhappiness you will put up with. Whatever your ceiling of expectation is, all of your beliefs and opinions support it and therefore you create your reality within those constraints. Your beliefs are the drivers of what you can and cannot attain. If you can avoid being told that something is impossible and therefore your mind does not fix on that belief, then you will be able to go beyond the ceiling of expectation of others. Here is an excellent example of how this has happened.

Breaking the speed barrier

On 6 May 1954, a medical student called Roger Bannister ran a mile in under four minutes. Before his victory, running a mile in under four minutes was considered one of man's hitherto unattainable goals. Bannister broke through a cultural ceiling of expectation. Because he proved that this sporting and physical achievement was possible, other athletes were also able to run a mile in under four minutes. During the subsequent decades, runners gave themselves permission to support Bannister's achievement, but I wonder how long it would've taken if he had not broken through that cultural belief when he did.

People like Roger Bannister stand out because they carry a level of faith and certainty that is unusual. Most people live life constrained by their hidden ceilings of expectation. It is important to identify yours and raise them.

You now know why it is easy to make ill-considered decisions that lead to wasted time, money and energy. Choices that lead to disappointment and disastrous outcomes. So we need a completely different way of making choices that will lead you to be able to live a fulfilled and successful life in a way you can only imagine. A process that means you hit the bullseye every time. I have developed a paradigm that revolutionises the old way and ushers in the new way of harnessing your consciousness to maximise your quality of life.

The Empowered Choice Cycle

It starts with a new cycle that replaces the disappointing outcome cycle. It is called the empowered choice cycle and I am now going to explain it in detail.

The empowered choice cycle

Sunflowers always face the sun

It all starts with a plant. The sunflower is a beautiful, huge flower with golden petals – or is it? In fact, what looks like the centre of the flower is a carrying platform for thousands of tiny flowers and they have evolved an ingenious way of getting the most out of life. Each morning, every single sunflower faces the sun and during the day they turn to follow where the sun travels across the sky. The big, thick stem that carries the huge centre twists itself around 180°. Recent research shows that during the night it twists back around fully, so that the sunflower is facing the sun again in the morning. This means that each and every tiny flower is always being bathed in the most light and nourishment that it can get throughout its growing season. Imagine living your life the same way: always being open and aligned to making the best choice in all situations? Always facing the sun.

The sun is the brightest star we can see, so I have called my system for living a life of no mistakes 'Bright Choices'. A Bright Choice is one that you make when you have the maximum alignment with the best outcome. By following the empowered choice cycle, you are able to make Bright Choices in every situation. There are three stages in the empowered choice cycle and I am going to explain them to you in detail next.

Deal with emotional baggage

Everything comes back to the Survival Calculation that our minds perform every second of our lives. The whole choice-making process is coloured by our past experiences. We carry the emotional charge attached to an experience and if we have not processed and dealt with unpleasant and distressing emotions, they will influence us when we are making a decision.

One of the most important ways that your mind decides whether a current situation is harmless or harmful for your physical survival is by calculating the crude basic factors of a situation. Emotional baggage can make you vulnerable to making disastrous mistakes. To give you an example of how that can happen, imagine meeting somebody new and your mind identifying them with somebody from your past who treated you badly. Your mind will tell you to beware of the new person because they are potentially dangerous. It could be right, but it could also be completely wrong. It could be the sound of that person's voice, the way they wear their hair, or what they say that triggers your mind to judge them as risky. Your mind has already made the decision, so if you hear a negative comment about that person from somebody else, you are much more likely to agree – because it supports your mind's reality.

This is often how group rejection starts and becomes a problem. The target is deemed a pariah by an influential person in a group and the rest follow suit because they want to believe the story they have been told. The reason they want to believe the story is because their minds are carrying emotional baggage that distorts their perception. The other members of the group often don't think for themselves, but just make a knee-jerk decision and rejection behaviour follows from that.

Other people's opinions and gossip can serve to strengthen our own wish to feel negative about somebody if we are already negatively biased because of a past experience. We can fall into the trap of allowing gossip to act as a validation for our unfounded assumptions. However, this can also happen the opposite way, when we blindly believe in someone else's abilities because it validates what we want to hear. That is why you need to get clear on what your feelings are about a choice you are thinking of making – and especially the people it involves. Getting emotionally clear will help you to harness the power of making a Bright Choice.

Remove your logical limiter

The second area you need to take care of is what you believe to be true about the situation. I am sure you have heard the saying 'what you believe is what you perceive'. It basically boils down to what you believe to be possible and what you believe to be impossible. Think of how Roger Bannister went beyond the accepted and expected beliefs that others held about the possibility of running a four-minute mile.

When I work with my clients, I spend time checking through several categories of where their minds can get stuck in a self-limiting belief. Self-limiting beliefs are like the speed limiter of a car. The car cannot reach its full capacity. Similarly, a self-limiting belief will prevent you from reaching your full potential and block you from exploring other possibilities. It is a logical limiter.

Some common logical limiters are:

➤ I don't deserve to be happy.

➤ It is not safe to be successful.

➤ I do not forgive others for what they have done to me.

➤ I expect to be disappointed by the outcome.

➤ I do not value myself enough to achieve my goals.

➤ I do not own my own opinions.

➤ I am a victim of unhappiness.

You may think these self-limiting beliefs are of no real importance. You may think you can just get over them or ignore them, and everything will work out just fine. What you need to realise is that most of these logical limiters lurk in your unconscious mind and sometimes you have no idea that your mind even holds the self-limiting belief. Your unconscious mind is where the blueprints for your view of yourself, others and the world are stored. Your behaviour is the result of the unconscious undercurrents of those perceptions. The belief ladder shows you why the quality of your beliefs is so important to the quality of your life.

The Belief Ladder

➤ Your beliefs determine your thoughts.

➤ Your thoughts determine how you feel.

➤ How you feel determines your internal state.

➤ Your internal state leads to the choices you make.

➤ The choices you make lead to the actions you take.

➤ The actions you take determine what you attract in.

➤ What you attract in determines the quality of your life.

Before you make a choice, especially if it is life-changing, make sure you have uncovered any logical limiters and turned them into a positive belief. This is the second vital shift that needs to happen before you can make a Bright Choice.

Your inner compass

I am sure you have considered your emotions and thoughts before, and it is pretty obvious that they can be great influencers in whether you make a good choice or one that turns out to be a disappointment. However, you may not be aware of the third part of what makes a Bright Choice a success.

Our bodies are wired for truth. This means that you have a high level of sensitivity that allows you to respond to environmental factors in the right way – that is, in ways that will support and benefit you. But if you are focusing on your mind and the thoughts that you have, it is likely that you are missing out on a wealth of data that is there to help you make good choices. Even if we are stuck in a state of denial about something in our lives, our bodies will be constantly giving us messages about the truth of the situation. That is why if we tell a lie, it doesn't feel good for the majority of people. It is the act of trying to change the truth and that doesn't work. It sets up stress and uncomfortable feelings in us.

Your body will always point north on your inner compass, and direct you to the truth. If you get good at noticing the difference in how you feel, you will know when a decision is right for you or not. By knowing this you have a tremendous advantage in making decisions. So how can you access this game-changing information?

I want to take you back to the beginning of this chapter, where I wrote about weaving and how each time a weft thread is laid across a warp thread a pattern is locked into the evolving fabric. Let's take a step away from that weft thread, to the moment before it is shot across and through thousands of tight warp threads. This is the point that weavers call the shed, when those thousands of threads separate in a configured pattern and a specific number are lifted up out of the harness. But what makes those threads lift? What I learnt about weaving during my textile design degree opened my eyes to the fundamental truth of what makes the difference between living a disastrous life and knowing what to choose for success. Now I am going to pass that illuminating insight on to you.

It all comes down to wooden pegs

I used to work on a dobby loom, which is an ancient contraption first invented in the 1800s, but which held the seeds that now enable you to scroll on your mobile phone and post on social media. The dobby loom is named for the dobby, which at the time revolutionised fashion because suddenly people were able to manufacture fabric with beautiful woven patterns. It is a selecting mechanism in a box that sits at the top of the loom.

The dobby loom that I had used lags. The lags determine the pattern as the dobby lifts them into place during the weaving process. Lags are small rectangular pieces of wood with a row of holes. Each lag is chained to a whole row of others. Each of these holes represented a repeating pattern in the design of the fabric. Along with the lags, I had a box of tiny wooden pegs, a pair of pincers and a hammer.

So what do you think I did with all of this? I had a simple yet deeply profound choice to make. Either I hammered a peg into a hole, or I left it open. If I hammered a peg in, the threads it controlled would lift. Equally, if I left a peg out, those threads would not lift. In effect, I was choosing to act or not to act. Each simple choice would determine what the fabric I wove would look like. But I had a powerful advantage in knowing what choice to make, because I knew what the pattern was that I wanted to create.

I mentioned that this process holds the seeds for how your mobile phone functions. That is because what I have described is called the binary code. Computer programming uses a code made up of 0s and 1s. Everything you can do on your devices today is due to this binary code. The tiny wooden pegs I was hammering in or leaving out were the 0s and 1s in the coding of the pattern of the fabric.

You use a form of binary code to make choices in your life: you either take action or you don't. Throughout this book, I will be giving you information to enable you to avoid making mistakes and instead make the right choices for yourself. You will discover how to develop a deep inner knowing and then use the energetic binary code of your vibrational environment to check whether something is true and aligned with the pattern you want to create in your life, or whether it is false and an anomaly. Always remember the lags and the pegs. When you can do that, you will be in the empowered choice cycle of making Bright Choices.

How do you find a needle in a haystack?

You've heard people say 'it's like finding a needle in a haystack' when they are looking for something they can't locate. But how do you find a needle in a haystack? Do you spend hours or even days searching every inch? The largest haystacks can be nearly two metres wide and a metre high nowadays.

I equate trying to find happiness and fulfilment without using Bright Choices to searching for a needle in a haystack. You can keep trying but just end up with more straw and no needle. Using Bright Choices completely changes the situation. It means you are suddenly holding a very powerful magnet which you can point towards the haystack. Now you are attracting the needle to jump out to you, wherever it is hiding. It means you are guaranteed a successful outcome as much as is humanly possible.

The ideal time and state to make a Bright Choice

You can only make a Bright Choice from a state which equals the least expenditure of emotional and mental energy. This is the state of inner balance, a balance between absence and presence, when there are no vibrations of feelings in your body or thoughts in your head. It is the pause between the inhale and the exhale. The moment where you can harness the incredible creative force residing within you. When you are no longer reacting with automatic or programmed reactions.

Instead, you feel calm, centred and balanced, and you can choose how to respond with full and free intention. You see the truth of the situation presented to you, without being influenced by any biased or distorted perceptions. When you make a choice from this place and you put your unbounded intention into what you want as the outcome, that is when you are completely aligned with the most life-enhancing solution. This form of intention is then like a laser beam: when it is sent out, it experiences no blocks or disturbances. The power driving this kind of intention is very strong and effective.

This is the ideal time to make a Bright Choice. The benefits are that you will:

➤ have a deep knowing that you got it right

➤ experience an immediate flow of energy and opportunities

➤ feel great with no doubts

➤ develop confidence in making future decisions.

In this book I am going to reveal the hidden organising structure that you can use to keep yourself from getting swept off course in the often bewildering currents of life. An invisible domain which is the vibrational database of all life. You and your greater consciousness permeate every part of it.

I am going to introduce you to the most powerful force you didn't realise you have. It will change the way you make choices forever!

Part One: The Vibrational Human

At the beginning of the Universe, when the Big Bang happened, a beautiful and life-sustaining dance began. This dance has never stopped throughout the history of existence – and it continues now. The whole Universe is dancing. Dance is movement, movement is vibration and vibration is energy. The dance is the constant exchange of energy between photons of light, molecules, atoms, rocks, plants, animals and human beings. In fact, everything in the Universe.

The chair you are probably sitting on is made up of the same stuff as the light illuminating the place you are sitting in. The only difference is the frequency of the energy it is vibrating at. The rate at which the dance is taking place. What seems solid is actually made up of the same stuff as the air that you breathe. If everything is energy, then our thoughts, emotions and physical bodies are also just energy vibrating at different frequencies. You experience the chair as seemingly solid matter because the energy dance is taking place at a similar rate to the energy in your physical body.

Hold out your hand and notice the matt shininess of your nails, the tiny wrinkles of your skin, the pale mauve veins running under the surface. You'll tell me it's solid; of course it is, it's obvious. But that is just one way of knowing your hand. If you put it under a microscope that showed your hand at a cellular level, you would see lots of round things, grainy bits, long thin bits, blobs and see-through strands. If you were to switch to a higher and higher magnification to a level smaller than an atom, you would see less and less stuff, until suddenly, you would see just wavy lines. This is the truth of your hand: it's made of energy and, in energetic terms, it's not really a hand at all.

So if we want to understand ourselves as human beings, it is time to look at ourselves through a different lens. The question arises as to what we are. There are many ways to answer, but I want to focus on the fundamental fabric of what we are created from. In order to do this, I want to open your eyes to some ground-breaking discoveries that changed our understanding of how we function.

But before we do that, I need to set the stage for you, so that you can see things through this special lens and you will know how to interpret what I am going to share with you in the rest of this book. The truth is that energy is a very misunderstood term. When I use the word, most people immediately think of physical energy – for running, for example; or perhaps gas and electricity, the sort of energy for which we pay a utility company. While these are certainly both forms of energy, they only scratch the surface of the energetic world we live in.

What is Energy?

The sine wave

The sine wave is the most fundamental form in which energy is represented. You may have seen it in images of brainwaves or a heartbeat captured on screen. Anything that moves or oscillates creates energy. A wave of energy has a peak and a trough, identifying the highest and lowest points of the wave. The wavelength is measured either from peak to peak or trough to trough. The frequency of a sine wave is calculated as the number of repeated oscillations per second. That number is measured in hertz, a unit of measure where 1 hertz is equal to 1 cycle per second. I will be mentioning this measurement throughout the chapters to come.

Energy has some other important characteristics that you need to know about:

➤ Energy cannot be created or destroyed. The energy that sustains life is the same energy created in the Big Bang. This is known as the First Law of Thermodynamics.

➤ Energy exists in many forms: thermal, light, mechanical, gravitational, electrical, acoustic, chemical, nuclear, atomic, kinetic and potential energy.

➤ Energy is transmuting from one form to another all the time. Electrical energy may undergo many transformations before it can power the light bulb in your home.

➤ Energy carries information in the form of wave-memory. Waves store information and have a way of transmitting it, which bypasses our notions of space and time. These energetic communications are instantaneous.

➤ Energetic information is constantly present.

You can now use this information as your travel guide as we step into the hidden world of energy.

Electrically Wired for Recovery

There are certain animals that are capable of regenerating amputated limbs. The salamander is one of these creatures. For a long time, this ability seemed like magic, but in the 1950s an orthopaedic surgeon and researcher called Robert O. Becker conducted experiments with the aim of discovering the salamander's secret. He became known as the father of electromedicine and electrochemically-induced cellular regeneration.

His research into the limb-regeneration capabilities of salamanders was revolutionary. He discovered that an electrical energy exists in living organisms, which is a controlling mechanism – and this energy is measurable and can be manipulated. He found out that there is an electrical control system that responds to injuries; when, for example, a salamander loses a limb, this electrical current network responds immediately. He measured the electrical currents that he discovered start, regulate and stop healing. In living organisms, the nervous system receives pulses of information via electrical charges and is capable of transmitting large volumes of information quickly. Even our broken bones heal through electrical charges: Becker put silver wires into broken bones, sent a current of electricity through them and healing happened rapidly.

When I broke my wrist, I had wires inserted into my bone to guide the knitting process. One day, a friend of mine who plays the didgeridoo brought his instrument round to play to me – and the sound gave me the extraordinary sensation of a vibration going through the wires inside my wrist! The Aborigines have known for 40,000 years that the low vibrations emitted by the didgeridoo are the right ones to heal bones, tissue and even muscle. To experience the power of sound on bone was incredible. My break healed quickly; and I had another helpful friend who revealed how prepared the natural world is for injury too...

My cat would not leave my side while I was recovering. She purred loudly for two weeks – as if she knew that I needed the sound. I am totally convinced that she did know instinctively. Investigators have shown that certain sound frequencies can improve bone density and promote healing, and because of this, cats are capable of immense levels of healing. They achieve this through their purr. The vibration of the sound a cat makes when it purrs falls into the 25–150 Hz range of frequency. Interestingly, the strongest sounds of the didgeridoo fall into the range of 50–200 Hz frequency, too. Just the right range for enabling and stimulating bone to heal.

Through his experiments, Becker found the blueprint for healing is electrical and works in a minutely accurate way with specific cells, influencing their function even in relation to other cells. Whether energy exists as electricity or sound, it affects our bodies. We are electrically wired for recovery.

The Importance of Light

'We know today that man, essentially, is a being of light.'
– Prof. Fritz-Alfred Popp, founder of the International
   Institute of Biophysics

Aren't rainbows beautiful? They have always been associated with abundance and luck. Just think of the myth about the pot of gold at the end of the rainbow or the Rainbow Warrior from the Hopi Indian culture. The rainbow contains all of the visible colours of the spectrum that we are able to see. I have mentioned before that some animals have evolved to be able to use light very efficiently. Now I want to open your eyes to how you use light in every moment of your life. Not only would you not be able to see the physical world without light, but you would not even exist without it.

In 1970, an astounding discovery was made by a theoretical biophysicist called Fritz-Alfred Popp. He was experimenting with the effects of ultraviolet light on specific molecules. When he examined the difference between two very similar substances, it created a conundrum for him. One of the two substances was called benzo[a]pyrene, a polycyclic aromatic hydrocarbon known to be one of the most lethal carcinogens to humans. There is an almost identical substance called benzo[e]pyrene, which, on the other hand, is less harmful. Both can be found in cigarette smoke, petrol and diesel exhaust fumes, coal tar and charcoal-broiled foods. The difference is a tiny alteration in their molecular makeup. Popp shone ultraviolet light on both of the substances and found two very different results. Whereas the benzo[e]pyrene absorbed the light and shone it back in exactly the same form, the benzo[a]pyrene re-emitted the light but at a different wave frequency. It was acting in a similar way to the Enigma machine used in the Second World War. It was scrambling information. The benzo[a]pyrene was seemingly causing havoc and confusion in the information stream of light. Equipped with this knowledge, Popp went on to accurately identify another 37 substances as having the capacity to cause cancer.

Popp also knew that something extraordinary happens with this frequency of light, which lies outside of the visible spectrum. Ultraviolet light has a short wavelength ranging from approximately 100 nm to 380 nm and it has a powerful effect on our cells. It is well known that prolonged exposure to the ultraviolet rays from the sun can cause damage to our skin cells and presents a risk for our developing skin cancers. However, it has been found in biological laboratory experiments that it is possible to destroy 99 per cent of a cell, including its DNA, by blasting it with ultraviolet light. However, when a weaker dose of the same light is used, that cell can be almost entirely repaired in a single day. The research suggests that a wavelength of 380 nm acts as a powerful activator in some way and interacts with the cells in our skin.

Popp wondered why a light scrambler such as benzo[a]pyrene acted as a carcinogen and realised that it must be preventing the ultraviolet light from being able to repair the cell. But in order for the light scrambling to occur, the light had to be re-emitted from somewhere. Popp started to toy with a startling idea: that our cells actually contain particles of light. He went on to work with a young physicist called Bernhard Ruth, who built a machine called a photomultiplier that could count individual photons of light. The truth began to reveal itself.

The two scientists began experimenting with seedlings. Day after day, they watched as living cells absorbed and re-emitted photons of light, even when the seedlings were grown in total darkness. They saw that when there was no light in the environment, the plant cells glowed even brighter.

So what do these findings mean for us as humans? We are made up of trillions of living cells. Do our cells hold light too? Popp and Ruth eventually started to examine human volunteers using the photomultiplier. They discovered that we too absorb photons of light into our cells and then re-emit these at very specific intervals. This is called delayed luminescence – and we are doing it all the time. This is one reason why, for example, we might say 'you look bright today' to someone who is looking healthy and why pregnant women are said to glow.

The amount of light we emit indicates illness too. Popp and Ruth found that when they monitored volunteers with cancer, the photon emissions were fewer and there was a lack of coherence in the natural rhythms of these. Those suffering from stress showed an increase of photon emissions; their system seemed to be lightening the load and working to find balance and coherence again. This indicates one of the reasons why we cannot make an informed logical decision when we are emotional: our rhythm goes out of sync.

Imagine one of your trillions of cells. You receive light from the sun. That light is absorbed by yourself. Your cell absorbs it as a wave of energy and in doing so, it unlocks the whole spectrum of electromagnetic frequencies that you need in order to live. In Part Three: Planetary Currents, I will be sharing just how incredible that electromagnetic spectrum is and why you have a symbiotic relationship with it.

Seeing the Biofield

Now you know that your body is subject to electricity and electrical fields that influence your day-to-day life. We have seen how if injury occurs, electrical currents immediately transfer information to your cells and start the recovery process. Let's shift our focus next to outside of the physical body, to observe how energy and energetic influence extend to beyond the visible realm.

In 1939, a Soviet engineer called Semyon Davidovich Kirlian discovered that if he photographed living things that had been exposed to a pulsed electromagnetic field, the photograph would capture what seemed to be a halo of light around the object. His discovery was the beginning of a revolution in new techniques to read and reveal this once elusive part of our beings. What he was seeing was the biofield, which every living entity is surrounded by.

In 1995, Professor Konstantin Korotkov, a Russian quantum physicist, became fascinated by the work of Kirlian and especially about his belief that the halo of light he had photographed could reflect a person's state of health. He developed a very special apparatus called the GDV (Gas Discharge Visualization) camera. With it, he was able to measure the intensity of light that a person was giving off. This was the same light that Fritz Alfred Popp had measured with his photomultiplier. It was now possible to see delayed luminescence emanating from the physical body and to record it on a computer. In his book *Energy Fields Electrophotonic Analysis in Humans and Nature*, Professor Korotkov states that: 'The physical aura of the biological object and man in particular is the total combination of the physical fields and radiations, formed by a body in space both due to its own emission and interaction with the processes in the environment.' I am sure that over the next few years, research will yield more evidence to help us to reassess what we truly are made of.

What is the biofield?

So what is this field of emanations radiating out from our visible flesh? The biofield is the electromagnetic field that extends several metres out from our physical bodies in an egg shape. It cannot be seen with a normal focusing of the eyes.

The biofield is partly composed of EM (electromagnetic) radiation, spanning from microwave, infrared (IR) to ultra violet (UV) light. The low frequency microwave and infrared part of the spectrum seem to be related to low levels of the functioning of the human body, including body heat, our DNA structure, our metabolism and circulation. The higher frequencies, including UV light, seem to be more related to our conscious activity, such as thinking, creativity, intentions, sense of humour and emotions.

The biofield is thus a complex and comprehensive database of ever-shifting energy, which is both recording and revealing what is happening to you as you live and interact with your environment. It forms an energetic landscape which is contained within the structure of what I call our 'energy anatomy'.

The vortices of light

Ancient cultures have long known that we are not just made up of our physical bodies, of those tangible parts of ourselves that we can see and touch. They knew about our biofield – the invisible structure that surrounds us in a great field of interweaving light.

Light and sound have a special vibrational relationship. Sound that is raised up many octaves becomes colour. Many hundreds of years ago, cultures such as that in ancient India knew that vortices of light form part of our biofield. Seven of these vortices have a close connection with our physical bodies. However, within the last ten years, others have become accessible to us and these exist outside the physical part of us, in the mid-range region of the biofield that surrounds us. They have become accessible to us because of the rising level of vibrations on our planet due to several cosmic factors and our own spiritual evolution.

All of the vortices act as energy exchange centres. They are spinning wheels of light where energetic information is processed, transmitted and received into our system. These centres each resonate with a particular spectrum of energy data, including colour, sound, emotion, mental perception and physical form. They are known as 'chakras', a term that means 'wheel' in the ancient language of Sanskrit. According to Hindu beliefs, everything in the Universe is made of sound. Each chakra therefore has what is called a 'seed sound' or *bija* mantra. These seed sounds are the symbolic representations of the energy pattern of each chakra and hold its essence. As you are made of energy, your thoughts and emotions also carry a resonance, a vibration.

The chakras or vortices of light are each activated by particular parts of the electromagnetic and acoustic spectrum. I work with 13 of these vortices and they form an integral part of your energy anatomy, the invisible energetic structure that makes up the biofield. The table below illustrates these 13 vortices of light, which you can use as a tool to check where you might be out of harmony in your life. Ignoring these energy centres can lead to our making mistakes, but our energy anatomy always gives us the correct and relevant information to help us make better choices. The 13 vortices of light act as sign posts and markers to keep you on track, which I will expand on in Part Two: What Lies Between Us.

Although 7 out of the 13 vortices of light resonate with colours in the visible spectrum, the other six resonate with frequencies that fall outside of what our human eyes can perceive, so in the table that follows I have given you the nearest match to a colour you'll recognise. Regarding the associated sound frequencies, the off-body vortices need more research and may be outside the range of our hearing.

Vortex of Light	Colour	Musical Note	Life Theme	Location
Earth	Dark red/ brown	F#	Shifting sands and grounding	30 cm (1 foot) below your feet
Root	Red	G	Belonging and tribal energy	Base of your spine
Sacral	Orange	A	Money, power, sex and control	Just below your navel
Solar Plexus	Yellow	B	Self-worth, self-esteem, courage	Stomach
Heart	Green	C	Love, relationships and nature	Centre of your chest
Universal Heart	Deep pink		Compassion	30 cm (1 foot) out from the centre of your chest
Transcendental Heart	Platinum		The energetic bridge between the 3rd and 5th dimensions	60 cm (2 feet) out from the centre of your chest
Throat	Blue	D	Communication	Throat
Third Eye	Indigo	E	Intuition	Between your eyebrows
Cosmic Third Eye	Pale lilac		Spiritual intuition	30 cm (1 foot) out from between your eyebrows
Crown	Violet	F	Expansion of consciousness	The top of your head
Halo	Gold		Spiritual love	30 cm (1 foot) above your head
Soul Star	Brilliant white		Illumination	60 cm (2 feet) above your head

The 13 vortices of light and their correspondences

Let's switch the focus back to your physical body. Your body is made up of trillions of cells and even they function on electricity. A molecule called ATP, or adenosine triphosphate, is able to carry energy and release it very quickly in your cells by converting chemical energy into electrical energy. ATP is vital for most cell functions because they require energy in order for them to take place.

The reality is that whether you look inside your body or outside at your biofield, you are an electrical being. The electricity that you generate and use affects your environment. You exist in relation to the space you occupy and the reactions you have, whether they are physical, emotional or mental.

Personal Energy Principle 1

Learn to switch off your mind: it is a tool and is not meant for the incredibly heavy responsibility we place on it. It cannot cope.

Have you ever felt that your mind is on the edge of exploding? That it is on a hair-trigger and you don't know what will happen if it blows? This is a common feeling and it is a cause of the fear, unhappiness and sense of futility that we have been collectively suffering from for a long time. In order to understand why this is happening, we need to get down underneath the level of our conscious thinking – below the thoughts about what we are going to have for lunch or wondering when our Amazon package will arrive. We need to strip back the layers of the mind and see it for what it really is. We need to become its observer.

Emotion, intuition, soul and spirit have generally been considered to be irrelevant for living a successful life. Feelings have traditionally been considered to represent weakness and something to be overcome or beaten. We have medications to suppress anxiety and depression. If we can't categorise or label something, then it is to be ignored or eradicated.

What I am describing is the playing out of how the mind operates and shows up in our world. The mind is focused on one thing only: your physical survival. This means that it is looking out for Number One. Competition, personal achievement, ambition and winning against all odds are the domain of the mind. The reason that it does not consider emotions to be relevant is because it does not understand them.

Let me give you a simple test to show you what I mean. Can you understand love logically? Take a few minutes to consider the question before you come back to reading this chapter...

TIME OUT

I expect your mind either went completely blank, or tried to justify that of course it understands love, but was unable to prove to you that it really does. I encourage you to try the same exercise with compassion, empathy, faith, trust and gratitude. You will find that your mind doesn't 'do' emotions. It is very important that you start to understand this as you move forward into becoming energy aware and living your life from a different place. This mental inability is why emotions are considered by many people to be dangerous, lacking value or something to be ignored and swept under the carpet. This is the signature of life in a mind-dominated world.

The problem with living from the mind is that it creates a finite perception. This is because the ego-mind dies when we die physically. It is aware of its inevitable extinction and therefore cannot comprehend anything beyond that point in time. So anything created from the mind alone will have an inbuilt ending, because that is the level of understanding which is built into it. We talk about business life cycles, exit strategies and clock time, linear time, time... time... time. Running out of time, being behind the times, we even say 'time waits for no man.' Your mind is concerned with keeping you alive within the amount of time you have to live. It is a biocomputer that is constantly performing one task. You know about it already: it is called the Survival Calculation.

However, your mind does not constitute your total consciousness. In fact, your mind can be separated out even further. Your subconscious makes up 90 per cent of your mind and that leaves 10 per cent of which you are actually conscious. By my calculation that means you are unaware of what most of your mind is actually doing. I further calculate that your entire mind may only make up 10 per cent of your entire consciousness. There are no demonstrable figures as yet because science has not developed any way of knowing. But if life is made up of recurring patterns, the percentage would fit.

I regard this 10 per cent of your mind as acting like a spokesperson for a company – the person who tells you that everything is going brilliantly well, profits are up and the public has no need to have any safety concerns. Behind the scenes the 90 per cent is running on old, often defunct and unsafe operating equipment that needs a serious upgrade! Our mind-dominated society reflects the makeup of our minds. And our institutions echo our mental landscape. So when the Survival Calculation activates, you are mostly only aware of the logical spokesperson. All you know is that suddenly you have the horrible feelings of anxiety, anger, disillusionment or a plethora of other unpleasant and alarming emotions.

In a similar vein, the IQ test has long been regarded as the gold standard of human excellence. When I was ten years old, I remember a very severe-looking man turning up at our house one day. He had brought a formidable file of papers with him. I had to sit down in our front room and work through a booklet with questions such as 'What number completes the analogy 8:4 as 10?' Or, 'What shape does not belong in this sequence?' Questions that were mathematical, verbal or pattern-oriented, and about classifications, spatial awareness and logic.

I am not a mathematical genius and I am not good at cryptic crosswords. My talents lie in a different direction. At school, I could not see the point of learning about vectors, bearings or complicated mathematical equations. I never considered basing my career on these skills. Rather, I have ended up running an enterprise which offers a solution to help people who have based their highly driven careers on those kinds of skills. They are often the ones who are carrying years' worth of unresolved emotional baggage, and who are suffering the damaging results of living with stress and the consequences of making poor choices. In the end, they cannot cope with any more of it.

What was missing from the IQ test that I had sitting in front of me at the age of ten were the questions about caring, compassion, integrity and understanding other people. As I turned the pages, I did not see any attempt to find out how loyal I was, how trustworthy or how good a listener. In short, my heart, spirit and intuition were left out of a test that was meant to grade my intelligence; a supposedly universal standard that would give me a mark designed to categorise me as a genius, mediocre or at the hopeless level. But this is just one example from a long tradition stretching back several centuries during which the mind-dominated evaluation of life developed, especially in our Western world.

It is only fairly recently in our history that our emotions have been considered to be vital to living a life filled with satisfaction. For a long time, duty and honour were the most important considerations. People got married for the advancement of their families, wealth and social status. Personal happiness was not considered to be the most important motivator for making major life decisions. Men often followed in their fathers' footsteps into careers that provided stability and planned prospects. Women were expected to be satisfied at home with having babies and taking care of the household. Emotional fulfilment was a little like playing the lottery: it was not guaranteed. People had fewer opportunities to make personal choices, but at the same time there was less pressure to be individualised.

When soldiers suffered from shellshock during the First World War, this was interpreted as being the result of a lack of moral fibre and cowardice. As if horrifying death and destruction were just something to be taken on the chin. Those who could not cope and fled were named deserters and would often be killed by the military, sentenced for execution during court-martials. Some countries kill thousands of their own men for not being able to deal with the horrors of war. Having a deserter as a relative condemned many families to be shunned, vilified and disgraced. It was only in 1980 that Post-Traumatic Stress Disorder (PTSD) was recognised as a diagnosable mental condition. Until then, in plain terms, men were condemned for something that they didn't have any control over. A strong mind and a strong stomach were the epitome of perfect manhood and emotions were seen as at best not required and at worst representing an outright failure to do one's duty.

As I mentioned, our minds are only part of the consciousness story. But what happens when we continually put our minds in the driving seat of our lives? What happens when you make the mind your CEO? Imagine that fictional company with all of that redundant operating system, which their spokesperson is telling everyone is perfectly safe and successful. There are glaring gaps in the company's procedures and resentment bubbles away under the surface throughout the business – just like it does with your unresolved emotional baggage and logical limiter beliefs. The resentment is ignored and the operational failings are patched up when they threaten to bring the whole company to a standstill. The best you can say is that the company is coping and hanging on by its fingernails. This is how many people get on with life.

Imagine there is an employee whose job it is to come in to work every day and do a routine job which holds no surprises. He likes doing that one job, he likes the minimum responsibility. He is actually exceptionally good at his job. One day, the CEO comes to see him and tells him that he is leaving and wants the employee to run the whole company. How do you think that employee would feel? He only knows how to do that one job, only wants to do that one job – and now he is expected to take on everything, including the failing equipment and the grumbling of the rest of the workforce. See him now in the CEO's big shiny office. He has been given complete freedom to do what he wants with the company – and what is he doing? He is gibbering in the corner, overwhelmed by the enormity of the responsibility.

Yet this is exactly what has happened: the part of ourselves that is fantastic at protecting you and keeping you alive has been made the CEO in our society. In the same way, when we put all of the responsibility for our lives on our mind, it becomes overwhelmed and cannot cope. So what happens next? The horrible feelings start. Anxiety takes root seemingly out of nowhere; you feel frustrated about the small things and you are plagued with a sense of impending disaster.

In real terms, your mind activates your body to respond to the perceived threat it detects. If it perceives a situation to be a threat, your sympathetic nervous system will unleash three powerful stress hormones into your bloodstream: adrenalin, so that your muscles can prepare for you to run away or fight for your life; cortisol, which metabolises glucose into your liver to give you the energy to fight or run away; and aldosterone, which raises your blood pressure to move nutrients and oxygen out to your muscles so that they can work at maximum efficiency. These changes literally take over your body. When you are highly stressed, you can't think straight. Your mind goes into a freeze response. If you are regularly overloading your mind by putting all of the responsibility of your life on it or overstimulating it, eventually it can't cope. An overloaded mind leads to chaotic thinking and an incorrect perception of the current situation.

But when you can eliminate the threat triggers and learn to switch off your mind, you gain access to a very different part of your consciousness.

Personal Energy Principle 2

Get to know your inner Yes/No. It is the key to releasing you from doubt and illusion.

O ur bodies are wired for truth. This is actually the greatest gift you could ever possess. It is the key that will free you from mind traps and enable you to bypass the Survival Calculation; instead, it will allow you to know the energetic environment of every situation. Having this key will completely change how you make choices in your life. By finding your inner Yes/No, you will be able to use this as your internal indicator throughout the rest of this book. But before I put that life-altering key into your hands, I want to open your eyes to our world and how it is really only us humans who get trapped in our minds' complexities of thinking.

The Smart Plant

Cleve Backster was a CIA interrogation specialist in the 1960s. But he is best known for hooking up a lie detector machine to a plant and discovering that it had emotional responses. At the time, he was merely curious to find out how fast the leaf to which he'd hooked the polygraph received the water he'd just given to the plant. Backster happened to be a world expert on the polygraph machine but even he was not prepared for what happened next.

Backster had been working in the polygraph lab all night. While watering his two lab plants in the early hours of 2 February 1966, he wondered on a whim if it would be possible to measure the rate at which water rose from the plants' roots to their leaves. He focused his attention on a dracaena plant because of its relatively tall, slim trunk and long leaves, and hooked up one of these leaves to a polygraph machine.

He then decided to immerse the tip of a neighbouring leaf into a cup of hot coffee. Nothing special appeared on the polygraph chart. If it had been a person he was measuring, the reaction would have indicated a state of boredom. As he continued to monitor the plant for another quarter of an hour, he suddenly had a thought. What if he burnt the leaf with a match instead? As soon as he had the thought, there was a dramatic reaction from the dracaena, and the polygraph-recording pen moved rapidly to the top of the chart! No words were spoken; there was no touching of the plant and no lighting of matches, just his clear intention to burn the leaf. The dracaena registered what could only be recorded as panic.

He decided eventually not to burn the leaf and as soon as he had that thought, the stress reaction dropped in the plant. He found that even when he thought about burning its leaf again, the plant knew that he was not serious about it, so did not respond again! The plant knew he didn't really mean it. It had the ability to distinguish between real intent and just faking it.

You Can't Even Lie to Your Breakfast

Believe it or not, you can't even lie to a pot of yoghurt! Backster went on to conduct further experiments into stress response; however, his test subjects were not people, but plants, eggs, yoghurt and human cells. He found that even the bacteria in yoghurt could distinguish a real intention from a fake one.

At the time, back in the 1960s, the idea that plants and micro-organisms had consciousness and intelligence drew derision from scientists. Only mankind was supposed to be blessed with that superiority. But here is the really ludicrous fact: we humans make more mistakes than something you put on your breakfast cereal! Imagine if you could live a life of no mistakes as successfully as yoghurt... Yet we are capable of being fooled easily. Just think about fake news and how successful it is in deceiving people.

Why We Can't Lie

Lying triggers changes in the body that we have no control over. Our heart rate increases and this alters our rate of breathing. The blood pumps faster, creating heat, and so we sweat. When our skin is normal, it does not conduct electricity as well as when it is wet with our sweat. A lie detector or polygraph can pick up on the minutest changes. The changes extend even further, though, because the energy in our biofield also reveals deception as there is a polarity switch in that energy. Just like the binary code, something either exists or it doesn't.

So why is it that our body goes through these changes when we lie? It is because we are trying to change the truth and that does not serve the body. Lies are always a shaky foundation for survival. The information is contradictory and this creates stress. When we feel stress our body reacts by releasing the three powerful stress hormones into our bloodstream that we touched upon earlier: adrenalin, cortisol and aldosterone are mainly responsible for those changes that take place when we lie.

Incredibly, even if you are in denial and unaware that something else is not quite as it seems, your body will still react, as it is wired for truth. As an example, you may feel something's not quite right about someone and your mind tells you that you are just imagining things. So you pay attention to your mind. But if that person is deceiving you, at the same time you will feel uncomfortable on some level, even if this is very subtle. So the vital next step is to get to know your inner Yes/No and use it as your dominant source of information from now on every time you have a decision to make.

How to Get to Know Your Inner Yes/No

The simplest way to start this process is with something you have no doubt about: your own name. We will use your name throughout this exploration.

➤ First, just say out loud: '*My name is…. [your name].*' Sit quietly and notice what you notice.

➤ How does your body feel? Do you notice any responding tension or a drop in tension? Does saying your name give you an emotional feeling or does it make you feel neutral? Does your heart feel open or closed?

➤ Expand your attention out from yourself and feel into how your name interacts with your environment. Do you get a solid feeling or a nebulous feeling? Do you sense a flow through you or a resistance? Does saying your name make you feel light or heavy?

➤ Now do the same exploration, but using a different name, one that is not yours; say: '*My name is… [a name that is not yours].*' Sit quietly and notice what you notice.

➤ How does your body feel? Do you notice any responding tension or a drop in tension? Does saying another name give you an emotional feeling or does it make you feel neutral? Does your heart feel open or closed?

➤ Expand your attention out from yourself and feel into how a name that is not yours interacts with your environment. Do you get a solid feeling or a nebulous feeling?

➤ Do you sense a flow through you or a resistance? Does saying a name that isn't yours make you feel light or heavy?

> ➤ Did you notice a difference? It may be quite subtle and that is because you need to practise. This is a new skill and as with anything new, it takes time to get used to it. But with consistent practice you will be able to cut through your mind chatter and feel the truth of every situation. You now know your inner Yes/No. You will be aware instantly if someone is lying or telling the truth.

One further step you can take is to actively use your body as a truth detector through learning the biofield sway.

The Biofield Sway

As you know, your body functions through electricity. Your muscles, your brain, even your cells are all powered by electrical charges. The emanations from the electricity that your body uses stretch out into your biofield and can be picked up as voltage through measuring electro-dynamic fields.

Harold Saxton Burr was Professor Emeritus, Anatomy at Yale University School of Medicine. At the beginning of the twentieth century, he conducted experiments into the voltage that the body produces. He discovered that a simple voltmeter shows that changes in our emotional states and physical illness cause fluctuations in the energy signature of the biofield. His research indicated that the biofield is responsive to our thoughts and life functions.

How to Do the Biofield Sway

I wanted to tell you about Saxton Burr's research so that when you give the biofield sway a go, you will be open to what happens.

➤ First, stand straight with your feet parallel facing forwards. Take the tension out of your knees. Gently rock backwards and forwards from your ankles to get the feel of this. Then come to a still point.

➤ Now say: *'My name is... [your name].'* Allow your body to do what it is naturally drawn to do. The most common experience is that you will feel a pull forward.

➤ Come back to a still point and then say: *'My name is... [a name that is not yours].'* Allow your body to do what it is naturally drawn to do. The most common experience is that you will feel a pull backwards.

➤ If you have any other experience – for instance, you get a reversed result – go to my website (using the QR code or link on page 8) and watch the video for further guidance.

Using this book, apply your inner Yes/No and the biofield sway to find out what resonates with you and what doesn't. These instinctive reactions will become your guide and your best friend.

Personal Energy Principle 3

Deal with distressing emotions as soon as possible. Don't
let them build up. They don't disappear, only get parked.

Have you ever tried to recall a memory and found it was just a
fuzzy, elusive fragment? Did you find the more you tried to get
hold of it, the further it seemed to slip out of your grasp? It can
be annoying not to be able to remember what you want to.

But imagine if your memories were surrounding you all
the time – in sharp focus? Imagine if you could record all of
your memories: the place, time, weather conditions, corresponding public events and even the way you felt, as if the events
were happening right now. Imagine if you lived your whole life
since the age of ten years old reliving all of your memories, every
day. How exhausting that would be!

There are people who live their lives like this. There is a rare
form of memory recall called HSAM, or highly superior autobiographical memory. For these people, there is no question that
they remember every single experience. They are the living proof
that nothing disappears, but just gets parked in our consciousness. In 2006, an in-depth study was conducted into HSAM and
the results were astonishing. Using a screening process, a large
number of individuals professing to have HSAM was narrowed
down to ten people. Researchers put them through a battery of
memory tests. These tests covered general cognitive abilities,
specific autobiographical memories and MRI and fMRI scans
focusing on four parts of the brain. Of the 115 adults who were
initially screened through a public quiz, 42 of them advanced to
a second quiz called the '10 Dates Quiz'.

Eventually, through a process of laboratory interviews, 11
participants were selected to go through a rigorous cognitive
battery of testing. These individuals completed an hour-and-a-

half set of tests, which included recalling specific categories of personal memories that they were given no chance to prepare for. They were encouraged to give as much detail as possible, such as weather conditions, locations, all the people present and also their thoughts and emotions on the occasion. All the information gathered was then verified with their personal documents and web searches. Even historical weather databases were checked for accuracy.

There was also a control group set up of individuals who matched the ages of the participants and who were put through the same tests. The results were highly significant. In the auto-biographical memory test, 10 out of 11 HSAM individuals scored 100 per cent with the 11th only making one single error! The results were a score of 33.91 for the HSAM participants compared to 11.33 for the control group.

Your Emotional Nessies

Loch Ness in Scotland is 230 metres deep in places. This body of water is famous as the residence of an enigmatic creature affectionately named Nessie. On 2 May 1933, a couple visiting the loch claimed to have seen a huge creature with a long neck. The encounter was reported in the local paper and then a London surgeon took a photo that would shock and intrigue the world. The famous image shows a creature with a long neck reminiscent of certain dinosaurs. Since then, there have been over 1000 sightings and people have gone to Loch Ness in the hope of seeing Nessie for themselves. But the monster is as elusive as ever and her existence has never been proved. In a body of water of such a depth, anything is possible. Beneath the loch, there appears to be a large fissure, which can be clearly seen on the images produced by oceanographic mapping – maybe it goes even further down into the Earth's crust? Nessie lives in the deep, hidden from us and tantalises our imaginations.

Our memories can be like the Loch Ness monster – such as of those times that were so painful, we have pushed them away from the surface of our minds and seemingly out of our lives. We think we have locked them away and that we won't have to deal with them ever again. But those with HSAM show us that it is not the case. Energetically, the vibration of the thoughts and emotions we experienced are still alive in our biofield. That is because we have not properly processed those memories and transmuted the pain in them.

Unprocessed memories can lurk in the depths of our consciousness, just like Nessie in the loch, and pop up when we least expect them to surface. Furthermore, just as Nessie is said to be wild, untamed and unpredictable, so too are our deep, rejected memories. The Swiss psychoanalyst Carl Jung stated: 'Painful emotions burden us. They develop from experience with trauma, loss, rejection, abandonment and failure. When we do not heal ourselves of these emotional wounds, neurosis can develop.' But painful memories cause pain if we talk about them and think about them, and sometimes that is too much to bear. The temptation is to act as if they never happened. When they surface and catch us off guard, sometimes we are not aware that they have raised their ugly heads. Suddenly we feel dreadful and an issue that is in itself small can rapidly turn into a major crisis in our minds. This is because we have allowed the energy of the emotional Nessie to amplify the current minor challenge. The monster takes over our lives.

Personal Energy Principle 4

Realise that everything that happens to you is created by you. There is no room for blame.

One summer, I was enjoying the early morning sun and looking at all of the gorgeous plants in my garden. I had a rose bush that grew the most beautiful scented red roses. As I held one of the flowers and inhaled the heady scent, I noticed that its buds were covered in aphids.

My grandad was the head municipal gardener in Budapest in Hungary after the war. He used to look after the gardens and floral displays in several of the hospitals there. He had his own plant nursery and he took me there once when I was on holiday visiting him and my grandmother. I remember being delighted by the riot of colourful, exquisite flowers growing on the hillside that overlooked the city. It was a hot summer's day and I thought it was the most beautiful place ever; I was nine years old.

My grandad was amazingly knowledgeable about plants and my early fascination and love for them grew even more on that day. One of the things he told me was that by soaking tobacco you could produce the most deadly neurotoxin on the planet and it was good for dealing with aphids. So when I saw the aphids I decided to go and see what was available at the corner shop.

I have never smoked and I was completely naive about what I would find. I asked the assistant to hand me the smallest packet of cigarettes, but I wasn't prepared for the nasty shock. As I looked at the packet, the first thing I saw was the image of a man dying of lung cancer and the words below said that smoking causes strokes and disability. I stood in stunned silence as the assistant asked for the money. I couldn't understand why someone would be buying something on which it was plainly stated that they were likely to become seriously ill and even die if they used it. I bought the packet so that I could sit and think about what was going on. In the end, the aphids lived happily on, as I didn't have the heart to harm them; the rose could fend for itself.

Why don't we respond to future danger? That was the big question in my mind. Of course, when it comes to smoking, the habit can be an addiction – but I wanted to see beyond that factor. The truth is, we are generally bad at protecting our health and no matter how dire the future predictions are from experts, many people don't do anything to help themselves. In the same way, how long have we known about the damage being done to our environment, yet the greatest threat to our survival has been treated with derision, contempt and complacency by so many people for so many years? The truth is, as the saying goes, 'it only gets personal when it becomes personal.'

A problem or pain only tends to become our focus when it starts hurting. To find the answer to why we can create huge pitfalls for ourselves, we need to go back to the Survival Calculation. You already know that your mind's number 1 job is to help you stay physically alive. That means it focuses first on what it can perceive now and, second, on what it imagines could happen later. Your caveman or cavewoman ancestor was constantly focused on present danger in a very dangerous world. Animals are always on high alert, even in hibernation, and naturally so are we when we sleep. We are programmed to deal with current dangers, not possible dangers. The future always seems to be a long way away if we are told danger is a possibility and even a probability in several years' time. This leaves us wide open to allowing disasters to mature and become real eventualities. We can claim we didn't see it coming, but how many warning signs did we actually ignore because our mind told us they weren't important enough at the time?

It is a very human reaction to a disaster to put the blame outside of ourselves. Newspapers are full of articles daily, telling the tales of people who feel hard done by. Sad stories that wrench at your heart. Almost all of them describe a situation that ends in unhappiness, loss and regret. The other dominant theme is that of blame. But placing the blame outside of ourselves is actually the greatest act of personal disempowerment we can do. The repercussions of blaming others are huge and damaging, and can lead to terrible mistakes. Blame leads to anger, distress, violence and devastating wars. Blame allows someone else to manipulate us into acting in a wild and unconsidered way where we end up hurting ourselves. We can quickly lose perspective and plunge into a dark abyss.

The truth is that everything has a beginning and that beginning sets the ball rolling for what happens next. So the real question is, how did we allow a situation to develop in the first place, in which we've ended up having to blame someone or something else for the result? What was our attitude towards ourselves and others at the beginning? What did we believe about the potential outcome?

Let us step back from our human lives – our day-to-day experiences that can be so confusing. I want to take you to a place where a scientist is conducting an experiment that turned out to have enormous implications for how we live our lives. I am sure that you have heard the phrase 'what you think about you bring about', or, 'what you believe is what you perceive' – and maybe you wondered what it actually means. It is easy to say it and point to the end results, but that does not explain what happens to lead to the outcome. However, when you understand what took place in that science laboratory, you will be able to fill in those gaps. Indeed, the answer will make you feel as if you have stepped into a sci-fi world, even though this experiment first took place in the nineteenth century.

In 1803, Thomas Young proved that light can exist as both an energy wave and a particle of matter. That was an astounding discovery in and of itself, because it shows that what we think of as being solid is often not that at all. But it gets even stranger than that. Let me tell you about the famous double-slit experiment...

Imagine a screen with two slits in it and another screen set up further away on the back wall. You fire bullets at the screen, one at a time. Bullets are solid, of course, so they will go through one or other of the two slits. You will see two bands of bullet holes in the back screen. That makes sense.

Now exchange the normal gun for a gun that fires photons of light, one at a time, at the double-slit screen. Change the back screen to one that is photosensitive and repeat the experiment.

You would expect the same two dark lines to appear on the back screen, right? Wrong! The back screen shows an interference pattern, just like the sort of pattern that appears if you throw two stones into a lake. The photons of light behave like waves of water. That is astonishing enough in itself because it means that each wave of light had to go through both slits at the same time in order to create that pattern. However, what takes the relevance into our daily lives is what happens next.

Imagine that you decide that you are going to spy on what actually happens to the photon, because it seems impossible for it to be in two places at once. So you set up a camera to observe the very moment the photon goes through the slits – and suddenly the back screen shows the same pattern that the bullets made! The photon behaves like a solid bullet instead of a wave of energy. How is that possible? Scientists are still puzzling over what happens but what we now know is that the observer affects the observed. So let's shift the lens back to how we make choices. When you decide at the beginning that the outcome will be good or bad, that is what you end up with. Henry Ford famously said, 'Whether you think you can, or you think you can't – you're right.' When you make a decision, you set events into motion to take a very particular path. This happens even when you are totally unaware of what you have unleashed.

I saw this reality play out vividly one day. I live near the beach and I was looking up at the wheeling seagulls. I remember hearing the keening call of a fledgling herring gull and as I looked across to the rooftop on the other side of the street, I saw a woebegone shape – stick legs pacing the skyline, up and down, up and down. Two parent birds were screeching the neighbourhood down, dive-bombing and hovering just above their chick. As I watched, the chick opened its wings, flapped wildly and then closed them again. If possible, it looked even more miserable. The screeching went up several decibels.

A few minutes later, another attempt, wild flapping, a bit of jumping up and down and a near miss from falling off the roof. Then the fledgling bird hunkered down and refused to move, despite its parents landing next to it and giving it an earful. Nothing happened for a while. Everyone took a break. Then suddenly it broke into wild flapping again, bouncing up and down, ran along the ledge and disappeared. The only indication of what had happened was that the parent birds' noise levels increased again, accompanied by frantic swooping. It was clear that their chick was filled with doubt about being able to fly, and so it couldn't. Instead, it landed on the ground. It took several days before it eventually got airborne.

In the same way, we are fundamentally responsible for everything that happens to us. By understanding this, we have access to tremendous empowerment. We will now be able to use this knowledge to make Bright Choices for satisfying outcomes.

Imagine that you have parked in a large car park and gone shopping. You spend a few hours out and about. When you are ready to leave, you return to the car park, but to your frustration, you realise that you didn't note down which row your car is in or where you parked it. So what do you do? You get your key out and press the button on the key when you are standing near a likely row of vehicles. Only one car will respond and it will be yours. Your key is coded to your car.

Now imagine replacing your car key with another key which I call a 'thought key'. A thought key is made up of your dominant beliefs about yourself, others and the world. Replace the cars in the car park with possible opportunities in your life. Now imagine pressing the thought key. What is going to respond? What and who are you going to attract? What will be your next experience?

Personal Energy Principle 5

Do not engage in dramas.

I have not owned a TV for about a decade and I have not watched the news for over 16 years. I made the decision when I realised that every time I turned on the TV, I was being plunged into manipulative fear and anxiety created around the Iraq War. I was planning my wedding at the time and I did not want my life to be blighted on a daily basis by the ambiguous reports of a nebulous aggressive campaign. After having my train of thought about wedding venues completely derailed by a particularly upsetting news item and feeling a sense of hopelessness for several days, I vowed I would stop watching the news altogether. I have not changed my mind since then.

My decision not to buy a TV happened when I moved from a rented place that had a TV, to buying my own house. It was the perfect opportunity to drop it from my life. This means that I have not watched adverts for nearly a decade either. Occasionally I have visited a friend's house while they've had their TV turned on in the background. Each time I have found it to be a great shock to my senses. I am no longer used to programme intervals where various products are paraded in front of me in the adverts, breaking my concentration with music that's often much louder than in the actual programme. I find it too harsh to have buzzwords fired at me from the screen.

Owing to not watching the TV, I am not numbed out to what is happening with my senses and emotions. In fact, being without a TV has been a huge eye-opener for me. It has revealed to me why we can get so addicted to watching it. It all comes down to security and disaster. Think about what happens when you watch a film. You have probably had a big build-up of pleasurable anticipation because you have seen the trailer. Maybe you have read the reviews and enjoyed watching the actors appear in other films. When you watch the film, you are taken on a rollercoaster ride of emotions. You feel suspense, romance, humour, the *ah! so sweet* moment. Most films follow a similar pattern called the Hero's Journey. The hero is any character who is faced with a challenge, such as how to win the love of their life, how to overcome danger or an unfair hand dealt by life. Our character goes on a journey filled with adventure and peril. He or she learns something or gains some vital treasure and returns a transformed person.

Next time you watch TV, notice how everything is set up to be a drama; even the news has its heroes and its villains, its damsels in distress, side-kicks, sages and everymen. They all have a powerful effect on your emotions. All of the characters I have mentioned are known as 'archetypes'. They are universally understood personas that immediately make us react.

The psychologist Carl Jung identified archetypes as: 'universal archaic symbols and images that derive from the collective consciousness.' They are the psychic counterparts of instinct. His Jungian archetypes are the Innocent, Everyman, Hero, Outlaw, Explorer, Creator, Ruler, Magician, Lover, Caregiver, Jester and Sage. You may recognise these showing up in TV adverts and news reports. Keep a notebook with you when you switch on your TV next time and note down how many of the archetypes you see appear.

Emotions are your mind's way of getting you to act. They urge you to either go towards something or away from something. Archetypes trigger your emotions and they create drama. A clever dramatist will lead you on the exact emotional path that they intended to.

Your logical thinking and emotional reactions do not take place at the same time. This is because, biologically, you either need to be planning what to do, or reacting to what is happening. If you are making a decision based on emotion which has overridden your logic, you are stepping onto the stage and into the drama. Your judgement can be impaired. Drama is your mind's dress-rehearsal for disaster.

And They Lived Happily Ever After

Do you remember the Survival Calculation? Drama is all about survival. If your mind can calculate, identify and protect you from all of the potential dangers you could end up suffering, then it has done its job. A happy ending means security for ever more. That is your mind's ideal outcome. In fact, even a genius like Bach was a slave to the idea of the perfect ending.

A few years ago, I was listening to a harpist at a concert. He would stop in between playing his songs to tell stories. One of those stories stuck in my mind. He told the tale of the famous Baroque composer Johann Sebastian Bach, who composed the Goldberg Variations. Sometimes he took on students to learn piano. He was quite pompous and, as a joke, his students would wait until he was upstairs in his drawing room and then play the scales on the piano but leave off the last note. The musical genius was so upset that he would rush down and play that last note. His mind hated unfinished patterns and had to have a satisfactory ending.

Personal Energy Principle 6

Get to know your own drama patterns.

Several years ago, I worked with a client in Texas who suffered from debilitating agoraphobia. She could not go outside, even to put her rubbish out. My client could just about manage to get from her front door to her car door – and that was the only way she travelled anywhere. Then, one day, her car broke down and she needed to buy a new one, but she couldn't go to any car showrooms and so she was stuck.

Our aim was to work together so that she could get over her paralysing fear of the environment. Part of my Life Retuning sessions covers the identification and elimination of self-limiting beliefs. I use the data in the biofield to accurately pinpoint a client's belief structures. I do not usually ask a client to identify them, but this time I decided to ask her to do an assignment. She was to write down all of the negative beliefs she held about herself.

The day before her next appointment, my client emailed me four pages detailing a tightly written list of what she had discovered about herself. To say I was shocked is an understatement. My heart went out to her, because this lady's mind was holding her a prisoner in her own hell. I want to share a couple of examples of the beliefs she wrote down:

➤ Nothing I do matters.

➤ I deserve to be punished because I am incompetent.

➤ I should never trust myself.

➤ I am not allowed to value myself.

As I read her list and saw the landscape of her mind revealing itself, I could not wait for the next day when we would begin to undo her torment. But one belief stuck me above all others. It was on the third page of her email, where she had written: 'I need others to be disappointed in me.'

I wondered whether this belief was more common than I had imagined. If what we believe is what we perceive, just imagine the sort of life this logical limiter would create. Exactly the sort of life where you would retreat into a debilitating fear, which would make you totally dependent on others who could spend their time telling you how disappointing and useless you are.

My client had grown up with a mother who could not bear anyone else stealing even one iota of her limelight. She made sure her daughter never developed any confidence, self-esteem or good feelings about herself. When her mother spoke to her, she dis-empowered her and left her with horrendous false beliefs about herself. I was helping her to undo it all.

Over the years of working on myself and with clients, I have uncovered some truly shocking beliefs that are held in our unconscious minds. We go about all day not realising that we can step into a yawning pit of error at any moment. Now, I want to unpack the belief we have about disappointing others to reveal how your mind is capable of tripping you up. You may be asking quite naturally how it is possible for anybody to build their life upon this belief. Surely it is illogical and self-destructive, you might be thinking. You are right – if we take things at face value; but as I have said before, in order to understand our behaviour we need to get under the surface of the logical mind.

The Devil You Know – and the Devil You Don't Know

There is a saying 'better the devil you know' and the natural continuation of it is... that it is better to deal with this demon than a devil you have no idea about. It is a powerful reflection of the Survival Calculation. The unknown is a threat to our physical survival – and that includes *potentially* good experiences, until we can *trust* them to be good. Even if a painful experience is painful, at least this is expected and we therefore know how it feels. This is one of the reasons why it is so hard to break out of an abusive relationship. As illogical as it seems, the pain we expect can be less frightening than uncertain relief.

So how is it possible to live within the belief 'I need others to be disappointed in me'?

If you grew up with a family member who let you know regularly that you were a disappointment to them, you may have developed a pattern where 'the devil you know' is others' disappointment in you, which is the 'better devil' because it is safe. You know how to deal with it. You might berate yourself for being stupid, lazy, not enough, not lovable and all of the other ways your inner critic can use to beat you up. But your mind is triggering the usual and expected response.

So what happens if someone isn't disappointed in you? Your mind will start off by being confused and then try to find a way to fit the unexpected response into the belief of 'I need others to be disappointed in me'. It cannot accept that anything outside of that is true and so it must somehow justify the fact that someone isn't disappointed in you. Typically, the next thing that will happen is a different level of inner critic starts up. You might recognise these kinds of thoughts:

➤ They don't know me well enough yet to get disappointed.

➤ They must be hiding the fact that they actually are disappointed in me but they don't want to hurt me.

➤ They are weird because they have not become disappointed in me and therefore they are untrustworthy.

Like a broken tooth that you can't help exploring with your tongue, you might be driven to test that person again and again until they have enough of your suspicious behaviour and reject you. Shockingly, you might end up feeling unhappy, but your mind will be satisfied that it was right all along.

In this manner, you may push away those who are caring and loving but who don't match your inner world-view. You may push them away because you can't have them around for that very reason. This can lead to you believing that all your relationships always end in disaster. That is because you are stuck in the disappointing outcome cycle. In order to change things, you need to identify what I call your 'Emotional Teddy Bears'.

Emotional Teddy Bears

'Available energy is the main object at stake in the struggle
for existence and the evolution of the world.'
   – Ludvig Bolzmann, Austrian physicist and
      philosopher

When I was little, I loved teddy bears. Dolls left me cold, with
their staring pseudo human eyes and plastic arms and legs. But
teddy bears offered a soft comfort. They had friendly faces
and fur, and I could cuddle them and feel better. I used to take
one particular teddy bear with me everywhere and when I was
travelling on the bus or train with my mother, I would go up to
fellow passengers and ask them to tell me what Teddy was doing!
I was inviting them into my world. I wanted the adults to join me
in my land of imagination.

Teddy bears made me feel safe and I could stay in my comfort
zone if Teddy was with me. So the term 'Emotional Teddy Bears'
refers to those reactive behaviours that make us feel safe. They
are the defensive ways in which we deal with the world. When
we feel threatened in a situation, we tend to display particular
reactive behaviours. These are most often learnt responses we
developed in childhood, when our mind decided what our defence
mechanisms would be. Later in life, when we feel outside of our
comfort zone, we automatically revert to our Emotional Teddy
Bear.

When we engage in reactive behaviour unconsciously, we play
out a drama pattern. As soon as we step into that role, we become
lost to ourselves and we let our behaviour take control of us. We
tend to feel separate from everyone else. We cannot see the implications for ourselves or others.

These are the six universal drama patterns that we need to
identify in order to become free to choose how we react to a
situation intentionally. They have two things in common: they
all reflect our deepest unnamed fears and they are all ways of
gaining energy from someone else in order to feel safe. The six
main Emotional Teddy Bear categories are as follows:

The Poor Me Bear

Gaining energy through demanding compassion from others.

When we engage in this behaviour, we are holding others hostage and wanting them to feel bad because we do. This is a way of controlling others by denying them their joy and contentment when they are around us. They often end up feeling guilty and responsible for our perceived troubles. If they are a person who has their own issues with feeling they are not good enough, we are exploiting their vulnerability.

This behaviour comes from a need for others to focus their attention on feeling sorry for us. If someone offers a positive solution, we may find ourselves rejecting it because we do not want to let go of our position of being felt sorry for. We may even push away those people who are too positive around us.

We need to take stock of what is really making us unhappy and accept responsibility for allowing it to affect our lives. To address the deep-down fear of feeling that if others are not feeling sorry for us and attending to our emotional needs then we hold no value for them. We are all valuable beings but only if we think that that is true. If we give up on our position of being the victim, then people will be much more likely to warm to us and want to spend time with us. This will then counter the deep fear we have of being of no value.

The Ice-Cube Bear

Gaining energy through withholding ourselves from others.

When we engage in this behaviour, we are protecting our hearts from being hurt. We have suffered such a significant emotional heart trauma that we cannot risk this happening again. Because of that fear, we hold ourselves off from others, denying them access to us and pretending to ourselves and to them that they do not matter to us. We rob ourselves of a deep connection with another person and the freedom to experience life to the full.

We can become very lonely and isolated through this behaviour. We do not allow ourselves to empathise with others or let them get to know us, in case they cause hurt to us through rejection, exploitation, control or obligation. We block ourselves from the effects of another person or make ourselves scarce when we feel in danger of becoming too connected. We starve ourselves of love.

This behaviour leaves others feeling confused, dissatisfied and questioning their own behaviour. We make them feel that they are missing out on us. We leave them out in the cold. Just because we were hurt in the past, it does not follow that we will be hurt now. The only reason we can be hurt again is if we think we will be. We need to focus on developing trust by letting go of past emotional patterns and opening up to those around us.

The Ever-Complaining Bear

Gaining energy through making others feel they are wrong.

When we criticise other people, we are secretly holding on to the fear that we are not good enough. We are all mirrors for each other and a constant negative judgement of others serves to highlight how unhappy we are with ourselves. By focusing on the perceived defects going on outside of ourselves, we can distract ourselves from addressing the uncomfortable issues going on inside us.

We are wasting our precious energy when we criticise. It takes a great level of courage to recognise what is really going on, to let go of judgement and focus on learning to love ourselves, but it is the only way to find contentment.

No one is more or less deserving than you. You can never know the truth of another person's situation unless you become them in the minutest detail. Don't ever rely on the biased opinion of another, but instead observe your experiences as you would look at a blank page: without engaging with any emotional or mental history.

The Bully Bear

Gaining energy through the fear and intimidation of others.

We often display behaviour that we have observed or experienced from another person. So it is with bullying behaviour. We have learnt that to get what we want, we need to make another person fear us first. We cannot rely on them to give us what we want from their own sense of kindness, because if that fails we have to confront the possibility that we have no power. We do not give others the chance to approach us of their own free will and through a natural attraction; instead, we take through force.

What is taken through force has no value, only what is given through love. It is the intention with which something is given that counts – and something given with love is the real treasure. We all have the ability to orchestrate our situations so that we can receive what we need and want without having to control others. When we start to show respect for another person and focus on fulfilling their needs, we will find that they are much more likely to respond to our needs as well. Then whatever we receive will make us feel so much better, because we will discover the truth of where real power comes from.

Focus on seeing the value in others and the ways in which they enrich your life just by being there. Refrain from looking outside of yourself in order to satisfy your needs and wants, and instead focus on generating the solutions from your own inner power.

The Drama Queen Bear

Gaining energy through creating anxiety in others.

All addictions are an attempt to numb our feelings of anxiety, frustration, guilt and other uncomfortable emotions. Creating drama is another addictive behaviour pattern. The underlying craving is for attention and the need to be seen as a valuable person who counts. The fear is that if we are not getting attention then we are irrelevant.

What if we turn out to be right? We cannot allow ourselves to experience a point where we are confronted with this question, because it is simply too painful to contemplate. The answer seems to be to make sure that people are always paying attention to us and our situation. The drama tends to get more extreme so that we get more extreme reactions from others. This is because, like any addiction, the substance to which we are addicted gradually loses its hit – and we crave more to cover over the underlying distress. The danger is that we can start to believe that everything has to be a drama and we may even start to embellish accounts of our experiences.

The truth is that drama takes place on a stage and is created by someone who is playing a role. Actors sometimes find it hard to divorce their acting from real life after shooting a film or being in a play that has a long theatre run; drama is exhausting to keep up and it takes us further and further away from the truth of ourselves. It can be very unsettling for others and their reaction may be to stay away from us, because they cannot cope with our behaviour. This only confirms to us that our deepest fear must be true.

We need to address our underlying fear of being irrelevant. We need to step out of the costume, get off the stage and operate from a place of authenticity. We also need to concentrate on listening to others and empathising with them. There is nothing more attractive than really paying attention to another person and seeing them for who they are. If we do this, we are likely to find people will like us for who we really are, too.

The Sell-Out Bear

Gaining energy through tempting others to give up their values.

If we grew up having our basic survival threatened, then the fear of not surviving becomes greater than the value of what we are willing to give up in order to survive. We lack trust that we are capable of surviving by ourselves.

What, then, are we willing to exchange for our survival? Once we decide this, we may allow ourselves to start selling ourselves out, which can become a way of life. We can be bought. Our silence, loyalty, love, ethics, integrity, morals and even our word can be bought. We allow ourselves to be corrupted – but where does it end?

We often don't think about our own or other people's boundaries and we end up putting others at risk too. If, for example, we tempt another person to break their commitment to their partner, we may be blinding ourselves to the wider repercussions of this behaviour, because we are only focused on our own security. Yet if we manage to lure them to stray, we will have been instrumental in the destruction of their own values. If that person breaks their word and then chooses to lie to their partner, they will have gone against themselves – which will lead to a deep level of disharmony within them too.

The behaviour of the Sell-Out Bear tempts others to buy what is not theirs to have. For example, you may be staying in an unhappy relationship or toxic job because you feel that you cannot afford to lose the security. But how much are you really paying in this exchange? It is like buying something on credit so that you can have it now but having to pay a high interest rate, which ends up costing you 10 times more in the long run.

You don't need to sell your soul. Once you tap into your own incredible inner resources, you will be able to provide for yourself and make the right empowering choices.

The Trouble with Teddy Bears

➤ Holding on to destructive and redundant behaviour

Leads to ➤

➤ Energy tied up in reliving past hurts

Leads to ➤

➤ Robbing energy from the cell tissues and organs

Leads to ➤

➤ Vulnerability to disease and lack of psychological growth.

It is time to stop your Emotional Teddy Bear from being your go-to state when you feel outside of your comfort zone. It is time to find a much better answer that leads to joy and satisfaction in your life.

Personal Energy Principle 7

Become adept at understanding the language of energy. Learn to feel with your biofield; it is your database of life knowledge and information.

Your environment gives you so many sign posts. Just as our ancestors knew to listen out for the alarm call of the birds warning of a predator, so you can learn to pick up on natural rhythms and signs. Part of these environmental rhythms are the energy interactions with your biofield.

Two Primal Forces of Nature – Ebb and Flow

When I go for a walk on the beach, I can hear the tide going out and coming in, ebbing and flowing. Ebb and flow are two primal forces of nature, constant and enduring. But what do they mean to us as humans?

When you walk along the beach, you can see that everything happens naturally. When the tide comes in, it is in a flow state and you can feel the power of the energy that is coming in, bringing the water onto the sand. We know how destructive high tides can be. We have all seen the devastation wreaked by the sea when the power of the water is driven onto the land. Even on a calm day, when the water comes in, it hits the sand and we can see the actual physical marks that the energy of the waves leave.

The other powerful force is the ebb state, when the water recedes from the beach. It trickles back all the way through the pebbles. It pulls right back and for a moment, there is a calm.

Let us look at the forces of ebb and flow through the lens of your own life. Because these two powerful forces are constantly at work within and around you. Energy is continually changing state, from one form to another.

Ebb state

Ebb state is where it seems that nothing much is happening. You may feel like you are wading through treacle, because everything you have planned and everything you want to achieve is somehow out of reach. You don't know why. You try this and you do that. You read, you meditate, you listen to *The Secret* audiobook – and for some reason you make no progress.

Ebb state is probably the most frustrating place to be out of the two states of ebb and flow. We can feel like nothing is happening – so what do we do? We grow frustrated and angry, because we can't see a way out of a situation or we can't find a solution to a problem.

But ebb state holds a lot of power; after all, it is a force of nature. If we understand this state at the fundamental level, we can use it in a very effective way. In ebb state, we can consolidate, we can learn and use this phase to heal. We can use this downtime to go through an internal transformation. We can use it for preparation.

Look at what is really going on if you feel in a state of stagnation. If you have something to shift, you need to go deep inside and find your core truth. What do you have to transform? What internal alchemy do you need to do in order to release yourself?

Ebb state can be transformative on the inside. But we might nevertheless grow frustrated, and then we will lose faith and lose trust. We can lose hope that we will ever get to a place where we will have our needs met, our desires fulfilled and our wants catered for. But this is precisely the state in which we can build up the power that we need to move forward, even though it doesn't always seem like it.

The reason it may seem like this is because nothing is happening in the third dimension of matter. But in the energetic realm a lot of activity is taking place, pushing you forward towards the goals and intentions you have set. Just because you cannot see this happening with your eyes does not mean it is not going on. If you use the ebb state and the power it offers in the right way, you will be ready for when the energy switch happens – when the ebb state turns into flow.

Flow state

When flow happens, you need to be ready. You need to recognise and seize the opportunities that are suddenly open to you. You need to be able to respond to what the vibrational sea is bringing to you.

But if you haven't used ebb state to prepare, you might not be ready and you may lose the opportunities. You might be filled with doubts. You may be lost in thoughts like 'I don't deserve this' or 'I am not good enough for this'. So you need to do the work in ebb state in order to be prepared for when flow comes.

Working with the energies of ebb and flow

What happens if you push at the wrong time? Imagine a boat travelling along a canal. When it gets to the lock, the only way through is for the lock to be opened and for the water on the other side to fill up the reservoir. If the water is too low, the boat will not be able to go through. If you tried moving it forward, you would get stuck. In the same way, the ebb state is when you need to fill up your reservoir of resources, whether that is mentally, emotionally, spiritually or physically.

On the canal when the water is at the same level on both sides of the divide, the lock opens and the boat can sail through. Likewise, you can sail through into the flow state and take total advantage of all the riches and the gifts and the abundance that are waiting there for you. In flow state, things tend to happen very rapidly, just as when the water is level on both sides of the lock, the boat can pass through without any obstacles.

Ebb and flow are very important to understand when it comes to avoiding making mistakes and exhausting our energy. So always check which state you are in right now. If you are in an ebb state, don't get frustrated and don't lose faith in the process. Don't lose hope. It may seem like nothing is happening, but in the background, everything is taking place. Things are being organised to align with exactly what you believe is possible. On the other hand, if you are in a flow state, don't procrastinate; do the work to make a Bright Choice and achieve a great result.

Your Energetic Landscape

To make the most of ebb and flow states, we need to have a better understanding of our own energetic landscape and our biofield. We have already seen how we come into contact energetically with the environment through our biofield – the electromagnetic emanations that surround our physical body and which stretch out several metres from us. Now it is time to take a closer look at what your biofield is made up of.

The Vibrational Layers of Your Biofield

The biofield consists of eight vibrational layers, ranging from the physical to the ketheric.

Physical: this is the third-dimensional body, which we experience as physical matter. It gives us information about the structure of our bodies, the anatomical parts. It is also where we experience the stimulus of our five senses and the feeling of pain. Your physical body vibrates at the lowest level of frequencies that a biological being can function at.

Etheric: this layer is connected to your life force. You may know it as *prana, chi* or *qi*. It holds the energetic imprint of your physical body. This is where the energy of the meridians are located which are used in acupuncture. In India, thousands of years ago, the meridians were already recognised to be pathways of energy that run through our body. There are 14 energy meridians. It is possible to determine whether a person's energy is strong or weak from this layer.

Emotional: this layer is where you will most often find the held patterns of the emotional component of your memories. Emotions are vibrations, as you know. They range from the most negative, such as fear, to the most positive, such as joy. This is the layer where these vibrations are most often found.

Mental: this layer holds the energetic information of your thoughts. This includes any self-limiting beliefs and perceptions you may have about yourself, others and your environment. It holds your ideas and mental processes. This is where logical thoughts reside, as opposed to emotions. Energetically, brain waves can be measured with an electroencephalogram (EEG). The activity of your brain cycles through several bandwidths of oscillations. These are categorised as Alpha, Beta, Gamma, Delta, Theta, Lambda and Epsilon brain waves. However, their influence stretches out from your brain into your biofield. Here follows a table listing the basic characteristics of our brain waves.

Brain Wave	Frequency in Hz	Characteristic
Epsilon	0.5 Hz	Suspended animation, reset of the brain and high coherency
Delta	0 - 4 Hz	Natural healing and restorative deep sleep
Theta	4 - 8 Hz	Relaxation, intuition, creativity, emotional connection
Alpha	8 - 12 Hz	Daydreaming and relaxation
Beta	12 - 40 Hz	Conscious thought, memory, problem-solving
Gamma	40 - 100 Hz	Learning, memory and information-processing and REM sleep
Lambda	100 - 200 Hz	Higher-consciousness state

Characteristics of human brain waves

Astral: energy vibrations travel inwards from your environment towards your physical body, where they manifest in physical form eventually. The Astral layer is where high vibrational frequencies of the outer layers of your biofield transmute down to lower frequencies, so that as human beings we can assimilate them.

Etheric body template: this layer mirrors the energy patterns held in the Etheric layer. It is like a vibrational blueprint of the physical body and the meridians. It contains the same energetic information of the body and the meridians, but translated up several octaves.

Cosmic: this layer is a mirror of the Emotional layer, but it transforms the active, visceral experiences of your feelings into energetic information of a spiritual and universal context. This context is no longer about your everyday life; it is connected to your higher consciousness. The vibrational frequencies at this level are several octaves higher than those of your actual emotional energy.

Ketheric: this layer is where universal energetic information and past-life energy patterns are found. It connects you to the soul level of your consciousness – the blueprint of your soul energy. It vibrates at a very high and fast frequency, and is not easy to access consciously.

Energy Behaviour

We all have certain character and behaviour traits. These are expressed in our emotions, thoughts and physical bodies. Our biofields similarly display behaviour traits, but these refer to how we assimilate and deal with the information we record from our experiences. There are two main energy behaviours: energy kickers and energy keepers. It is helpful to get to know what yours is.

Energy Kickers

This is the way in which some of us deal with the memory of unpleasant situations or trauma energetically. If you are someone who doesn't give yourself time to process an upsetting incident then you are likely to be an energy kicker. You just want to get on with life and you cope. Maybe you feel that a lot of people rely on you to be the strong one; the one who always has the solutions. You are likely not to dwell on the past and perhaps do not feel you have any time for it. You may not even be able to remember specific times clearly.

I have found from my client work that energy kickers store wave memories in the outer layers of the biofield. Often, this means that they have little awareness of pain from the past. But past distressing emotions do not disappear, they just get parked as energy vibrations in the biofield. If you are an energy kicker, you may have found that you have felt fearful or anxious seemingly out of the blue. You have no idea why. This is because, as an energy kicker, you swept the problem under the carpet long ago and now it has triggered in your life again.

Energy keepers

This is the other way we can deal with memories and emotions. An energy keeper usually has a very good memory of the past, especially traumatic times. The energy of those memories is kept close to the physical body and can even remain as a vibration in the body.

If you are an energy keeper, you probably relive past pain as if it were happening now. Often, this means that you will feel the emotions of a memory deeply and that you cannot let go of your thoughts about it. You may become re-traumatised regularly if you keep activating the wave frequency of the energetic information of those memories. You probably experience intense physical sensations as well.

I have found through my work with clients that energy keepers often have an underlying reason for keeping a painful memory alive. This may be conscious or subconscious and can be connected to a need for psychological protection. The other reason has to do with punishment and I will be expanding on both of these themes in Part Two, the Relationship Energy Principles section. Both reasons stem from the mind's need to remember.

Once you get to know your extended self and start to pay attention to it, you can harness that wider range of information to make good decisions; that is, to make Bright Choices.

Personal Energy Principle 8

Learn to take every decision down to your heart. Your heart will only give you the truth, because it is aligned to your energy – and energy never lies.

We have looked at the mind traps that you can fall into when making a decision if you listen to your thoughts above everything else. Indigenous peoples know the danger of living this way. They know that it is our hearts that are the centre of our lives. As I have explained, your mind thinks in finite terms because the ego dies when the physical body dies. Your heart, however, operates in a very different way. It understands the infinite nature of existence and doesn't question it. I heard a wonderful quote once that sums up the difference: 'The mind knows no answers and the heart knows no questions.'

If you think about it, your mind is never 100 per cent certain because a new experience can change your perception. The mind is like a butterfly: it settles for a while but the slightest disturbance can send it off into flight again. Your heart, on the other hand, is connected to the energy matrix – that sea of electromagnetic vibrations that permeates everything in our Universe. It is the storage of the memory of everything. Your heart knows infinity.

I want to reveal to you how incredible that energetic relationship between your heart and the energy matrix is. I want to explain why, when you live from your heart, everything flows and harmonises.

Living from the Heart

'Do as your spirit, your heart directs. Don't think too much...
when it comes to most things in life, the heart has the voice
to listen to, because the heart knows how to follow the
advice of the spirits. Your heart is part of the Universe. If
you listen to your heart, you hear the Voice of the Universe
or the Voice of the Soul. We only have to listen.'
– Tampur, Shuar Indian Tribal Elder[1]

Your heart has an electromagnetic field which not only envelopes
every cell of your body, but extends out in all directions in space
around you. Measurements done comparing EEG and ECG
results show that the energy of your heart is 5,000 stronger than
that of your brain.

The shape of your heart's electromagnetic field is very special. It
is called a 'toroidal' field, which means that it is shaped a little like
a doughnut, but instead of a hole in the middle it has a central core.

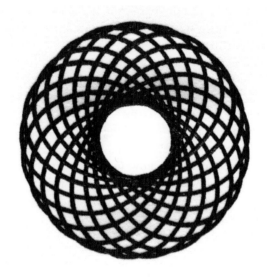

A toroidal field

---

1 Quoted in *Shapeshifting* by John Perkins (Destiny Books, 1997).

The toroidal field is a self-generating energy system. It has dynamic flow, which means that the way it uses energy is sustainable and eternal. Energy flows in through the central core and keeps on cycling out around the ring and then back through the core. Inside the core is where we find perfect balance – and that is where our heart is located within its own electromagnetic field.

As you know, energy carries information, and the shape of the heart's energy field means that information is constantly being fed into the core of the torus and therefore into your heart. Through your heart, you are constantly informing your environment of yourself and the environment is constantly informing you of itself. Through your heart, you are influencing everything and everything is influencing you in a state of perfect harmony and wholeness.

The torus exists everywhere in nature – from atoms to apples, from hurricanes to oceanic systems. The magnetic field of Earth is a torus and our sun has a torus field called the heliosphere. You even find torus fields in distant galaxies around stars. Your heart is part of the Universe – just as the Shaman Tampur says in the quote above.

Even on a physical level, your heart is not quite what it seems. Research shows that it is not just a simple pump, but has its own nervous system. Scientists have discovered neurons or nerve cells deep within the heart tissues. Neurons are the physical part of you that enable you to store your long-term memories. They use electricity to create connections and were once only known to enable thought processes to take place; until recently, it was thought that these types of cells could be found only in the brain. However, it is well known that some heart transplant patients can take on the feelings, desires and even memories from their donor.

Maybe just reading about this is already helping to make sense of how you remember experiences. Our minds deal with data and our thoughts are data. Our hearts, on the other hand, deal with feelings. These are two different languages and they need to synergise to create harmony. When we make the mind dominant in our lives, we cut ourselves off from the greatest part of ourselves. Living through your mind means you are existing, whereas living through your heart means you are truly living.

For many centuries, we have followed the Latin dictum *cogito, ergo sum*: 'I think therefore I am.' I believe it is time to revise this and bring our hearts into the centre of our lives. Your heart sends information to the brain through its heart field. It is your brain that synchronises with your heart, not the other way around. Your emotions are created by the wave structure of the electrical field of your heart. Your heart is also the place where your soul and intuition are connected, so if you feel confused or depressed, the most empowering thing you can do is to start listening to your heart.

Simply put, your heart is the energy dynamo that powers your life and connects you into the eternal database of universal knowledge.

The toroidal field of your heart stretches out in a huge electromagnetic expanse from your physical body. It is a connector field, which means we can also influence each other powerfully through our hearts (see the section 'Separator and Connector Emotions', p112). So what happens when we encounter the heart field of someone else? Studies show that the energy that we send out can create coherence in the other person. Let's take a closer look at what I mean by this.

Coherence

Coherence is a very important concept to understand. Imagine a shoal of fish in the ocean. A vast mass of thousands of little sparkling bodies. Look at how they behave. The shoal is made up of individual fish, but they move as one big fish. When one turns, all turn, continuously moving with flashes of colour and light coruscating across the surface of the whole of the shoal. How do these fish stay in perfect sync?

Or think about a flock of starlings as they swoop and dive together in vast flocks called murmurations. They form spectacular shapes across the sky. They are responding to the electricity they all share. They are in a coherent state; every individual is also a part of the whole.

The energy in your body and your biofield is similarly interlinked by electromagnetic fields. Coherence means to be in sync: our energy waves are in phase, everything is aligned and working as one system. Our hearts are not just capable of being in coherence but also influencing every cell in our bodies to be coherent too. When making a Bright Choice, this is the state that is the most beneficial for arriving at incredible and fulfilling outcomes.

MindFULLness vs. heartFULLness

In order to get to this state of coherence it is therefore important to deal with your emotional baggage and logical limiters. Your mind can create chaos and disharmony because of the Survival Calculation, but your heart can bring you into a state of balance, harmony and limitless access to everything you need to feel and know. So aim to quieten your mind and start listening to your heart. Only make decisions with your heart as the dominant influencer in your life.

Personal Energy Principle 9

Learn to love yourself as a whole, beautiful and valuable being. Make this your No.1 priority, as everything else flows from there.

If you spend your time listening to the media and other people, you can easily develop the belief that there is something wrong with you; for example, you might come to believe that if you are not size 0 then you are too fat; that if you are single then you should be in a relationship; and if you are not pushing to get a house, a family, a career then you are not doing well enough. *Blah, blah, blah* – it goes on and on. I want to bust through all of that and tell you the truth about you. When you were born, this world received a gift that it was missing.

Throughout this book, I have been telling you about yourself. I have been reconnecting you with your bioenergetic birthright. The truth is, if you are not satisfied with something about yourself, you have the power to change it in a heartbeat. Nothing is set in stone: energy is mutable. But it is your right to make that decision and not someone else's. My aim is to free you up from those influences that are not helpful for you, and to enable you to live an extraordinary life by making Bright Choices. So let's look at one way in which you might get caught up in someone else's life and become addicted to things that can pull you off track.

The Glamour Factor

When we have a deep need within us for which we cannot generate a solution or find fulfilment, we may get hooked in by someone who appears to have what we lack. Most of the time, this is based on illusion and we are comforting ourselves with a feed-line that is seemingly giving us what we cannot find in ourselves. The problem arises from the fact that we are not seeing the other person clearly, so we build up expectations that they may fall short of. However, the fantasy takes on such a potency that it becomes an entity in itself and often has nothing at all to do with the person we crave. This is what I call 'glamour'.

If we do not get to a place where we can see the other person for who they really are, and find the nourishment we need within ourselves, it can become very difficult to get over our addiction to somebody else. What we crave so desperately to be is fed by the fantasy, and because none of it is real we may feel a terrible hole that can never be filled. Whether it is to be cool, attractive, popular, smart, sexy, sorted or supported, the craving is constant and obsessive. The pain can become almost unbearable when what we lack shows up as a raw need, and when the other person reminds us of that lack and need whenever we think about them or see them.

A typical case of this happens with social media influencers, musicians and actors. They often become someone else on stage or on social media and take on an almost mythical persona. This can be a very potent drug for anyone who has issues with their own self-confidence, self-worth or self-love. Even a remote association with a desired celebrity seems to confer an illusion of worth and attractiveness. How can you give that up, even if deep down inside you know it is a case of Scotch mist?

The answer lies in concentrating on finding the root of the lack in your own life and perception of yourself. Once you can start to experience self-confidence, self-worth and self-love, you will realise the difference. Your feelings will become real and contrast sharply with the illusion you have based around the person you are hooked into. You see them for who they really are – and often what shows up in sharp focus is just how insecure and lacking they are too. They may need to be spinning the illusion around themselves, because deep down inside they are terrified that they are worth nothing. Fame can be the loneliest place.

How Do You Speak To Yourself?

Words carry power and can shape our reality: in Part Three of this book, the Global Energy Principles section, I will tell you how we know that energy vibrations leave a mark in our physical world. The soundwaves of your voice and the brainwaves of your thoughts all create an impression that shapes your future. So a good indicator of how healthy your energy frequencies are lies in how you speak to yourself and how you talk about yourself to others. Take a moment to consider this now by answering the following questions:

➤ Do you allow your inner critic to criticise you?

➤ Do you allow your inner whip-master to put constant pressure on you?

➤ How hard are you on yourself?

➤ If you spoke to the person you love most in the world in the same way as you speak to yourself, would you see joy or pain in their eyes?

Become aware of the words that you use in your mind about yourself. Actively start replacing negative words with positive ones.

Own Your Own Throne

A ruler sits on a throne. Symbolically, your throne represents your own seat of power over your life.

➤ I would like you to imagine that you are sitting on your throne. Do you feel comfortable or overawed by your position?

➤ If someone were to enter the throne room and walk straight up to you, would you have an overpowering urge to vacate the throne and let them take your place? Would you feel you are not worthy, a fake and not entitled to be there? Would you stand there feeling small, unimportant and diminished? Ignored?

➤ Do you ever find yourself in situations where your right to be there is challenged? Or where your right to lead, suggest, initiate, create or express yourself are tested by others?

➤ Have you ever found yourself being sociable in a group situation, when someone enters whose intention it is to take over the great conversation you are having? A forceful personality who wants to dominate? Who seems to have marked you out to sideline you...? How do you deal with this? Do you fume inside and feel disempowered – but secretly, somewhere deep inside, sense that they have more of a right than you have to the limelight?

If you are resonating with what I am describing, then it is time to own your own throne. It is not possible to make great decisions when you do not own your own throne.

As human beings, we take up physical and energetic space in this world. We are also territorial and power plays happen all the time in social dynamics. Become aware of what energy you are bringing into any space that you occupy, especially if you find yourself in a social group. If you realise you have the urge to 'step off your throne' when your place is challenged, ask yourself why that is. Are you holding on to a disempowering story about yourself in the belief that you are not good enough?

There are two kinds of people: those that life happens to and those that happen to life. Which kind do you want to be?

Put Yourself at the Centre of Your Life

When you travel by airplane, the cabin crew always do a vital thing. Just before take-off, they instruct everyone in the flight safety procedures. A flight attendant talks passengers through the exit and emergency points. Then you are told about the oxygen mask that is tucked away above your head. You are told that, in the case of an emergency, you need to use the mask on yourself before you attempt to help family members or anyone else. This is because if the pressure drops in the cabin, you will start to lose consciousness in seconds; a demonstration by NASA showed that you would lose your ability to recognise faces, feel unable to save yourself and eventually pass out. That is why this analogy is so powerful for what you are doing in your own life. If you have passed out, you cannot help anybody, not even yourself. If you are not OK with yourself, you will pass that on to other people. If you are OK with yourself, you will pass that on to other people.

In order to be able to make great choices for yourself, you need to undo what is stopping you now from doing that. You need to prioritise having a wonderful and healthy relationship with yourself. You will then have a balanced, harmonious and accurate understanding of each situation, without any distorted views.

Now is the time to dig deep and think about how you value yourself. As you value yourself, so will others value you. A good exercise is to write a list beginning: '*I bring value to the world by…*'

When you put yourself at the centre of your life, everything flows from you. When you nourish yourself first, you will have plenty with which to nourish others. When you fill your own heart with loving kindness and appreciation of yourself, you will have a deep well of love for others. Love is a vibration and when you are resonating at that frequency, it emanates out into the world. Build your own strong foundation of inner resources and you will not be needy. You will have eliminated one of the most common ways to end up in the disappointing outcome cycle.

Personal Energy Principle 10

When you act in an unconscious way, you are building up karma to work through in your next lifetime. Act the drama, create the karma.

Karma is a Sanskrit word that means 'action'. It is often a misunderstood term, because it becomes linked to the idea of punishment. But that is a human way of looking at it. Karma is not polarised into good or bad; it is simply the universal and vibrational consequence of our thoughts, deeds and actions. Karma is not a judge, it is a mirror. No matter when we make a choice, the energy of the intention we made it with will be reflected back to us. When I say 'no matter when', I mean that there are no boundaries in time beyond your physical birth. I am going to be expanding on this curious sentence very soon.

On another level, karma refers to the lessons within the 'work' we have ahead of us. Imagine sitting in a school room with an exam paper on the desk in front of you. You have to attain a specific score in order to pass. On the first attempt, you hand in the paper and walk out of the room. Your paper is marked but you don't achieve the pass mark. What happens now? You find yourself back in the room at the same desk with the same paper in front of you. When you do finally achieve the required score, everything disappears. You will never have to sit that exam again. In reality, the exam paper has no time limit on it and can come back to you at any time during your existence, if you have not passed it.

Acting the Drama

'[W]e have more than one incarnation because there are many themes and it is impossible to learn them fully in one life. Incarnations continue until each of us completes the manifestation of all the themes of the human monad.'
    – Dr Amit Goswami, *Physics of the Soul*

So where does drama come in to karma?

We looked at some common Emotional Teddy Bears on pages 80–85, and saw how we may get caught up in unconscious and reactive behaviours, thoughts, emotions and actions; and how drama pulls us away from our core truth and essence. When we act reactively, we create disharmonious vibrations; and, as you know, energy cannot be created or destroyed, and is therefore an everlasting recording of everything that has happened, is happening and can happen potentially. The quality of our intentions is therefore what carries through and determines whether we will have to sit that exam paper again at some point in time.

This is why when you make a Bright Choice, you are ensuring that everything is aligned and ideal. Because you are making a choice from a place of conscious awareness. You are not engaging in negative energetic patterns.

My own awareness of karma

'If everything is energy and energy is everything, then every experience, every thought, carries with it an energy, a frequency that never dies, never goes away, but exists in an eternal and infinite realm.'
– David Moorhouse, former US Army Ranger and author of *Remote Viewing*

Over the years doing the work that I do, I have realised that karmic energy patterns have a bearing on a daily basis and that we could very well be influenced to some extent by our past-life experiences all the time. For example, I was brought up in a religion that taught the concept of heaven and hell – a dogma which held that reincarnation does not exist. And yet from a young age I always had a strong knowingness that something was not quite right about the doctrine. Things did not go far enough. While I was controlled by the threat of eternal damnation for carnal sins, this never sat right with me somewhere inside.

What my own knowingness told me is that souls have to go through tests that will cleanse them until they reach a state of total purity and eternal bliss – and that they really have to work at this. I knew that this could only be achieved over several lifetimes, yet my religion denied this could be a possibility. To me, this truth was always crystal clear and made perfect sense.

Interestingly, it was a ruler who wanted to weld together his empire who threw reincarnation out of the Bible. It happened at the Council of Nicaea in AD 325, when Emperor Constantine decided to delete any mention of it and declared it to be a heresy. It begs the question: why was it accepted before his veto?

As I grew up, my thoughts and deep knowingness were overlaid with suffering through my making poor choices and the standard human condition of fear. My instinct about reincarnation became cloudy, until I reached a point where I no longer had a connection with my wise Higher Self. I lost touch and lost my way. I fell into a darkness of the soul and suffered the consequences. Our Higher Self, however, is always sending us reminders of who and what we truly are and where truth lies under the veneer of human illusion.

As children, we are taught by adults who think they know better than us that we cannot see biofields or spirit, or predict the future, and that memories of another life are simply the product of an overactive imagination. Gradually, we become conditioned into seeing the illusionary world, constructed long before we were born. We are taught to see what is not there and to ignore what is. As I became older, I was confronted by a situation in which I had to make a choice to take the blue or red pill: to carry on living in uncomfortable amnesia, or to rediscover the truth that I had known as a child.

I had always declined regression because I was scared of what that particular Pandora's box might unleash. I had read many articles about strange experiences where people 'remembered' that they used to be the Queen of Sheba or another famous person. I didn't believe these stories and assumed that these individuals just wanted attention. Then, one day, a hypnotherapist friend asked me if I would like her to regress me. She was on a training course and she needed a volunteer. I had no time to think about it, because she only had a couple of hours to spare – and it had to be now! I chose the red pill and so began my reconnection with reality...

I remembered my last life as a soldier, keeping the peace in the Middle East at the beginning of the last century. I recalled historical information that I had never read about and yet, when I researched it afterwards, it turned out to be accurate. I remembered this life so exactly that for the next few days I was confused as to which lifetime I was living in! It was truly weird. And no, I was not someone famous or distinguished; I was a common person who seemingly did not achieve anything of significance or make an outstanding contribution to the world.

My wider consciousness had broken through years of built-up misinformation. This experience led me to wonder whether, given that I had had a life before this one, it might be possible that I had had countless others before that. I became intrigued and started to consider the question.

I wondered whether it is possible to use hypnotherapy to access a person's superconscious mind through a trance state, whether there is another way to find out that sort of information instantly from the biofield. I reasoned that if we have a vibrational database, which contains the resonance of our thoughts and feelings, then it should be possible to 'read' our biofield. Furthermore, if energy cannot be created or destroyed, then all of the data of our past incarnations must be stored from the beginning of our existence. Therefore, it followed that it ought to be possible to access any piece of that information at any time.

I had already been working with clients on their current-life traumatic memories and distressing emotions. My results were correlating with a client's experience and improvement for issues in this lifetime, so I had a good starting point for asking questions from further back. The energetic imprints of the memories were there, just not held in the conscious mind.

One disturbing outcome of past-life regression was that I

recalled and re-witnessed a horrific incident. I watched someone being hanged as if I were there again. The image would not leave me – and my friend could offer no answer as to how to let go of it. I now understood my trepidation during the years when I'd refused to try past-life regression. What was I to do? This made it personally vital that I found out if my own system could eliminate this past-life trauma. It became one of my important breakthroughs in creating this powerful system, as I found the way to deal with past-life trauma without having to relive and re-traumatise someone. A safe way of releasing the past.

I successfully neutralised the upsetting images of the hanging in my mind; the vision disappeared completely. As I delved deeper into the past-life information, I discovered a whole other set of energetic patterns which I realised were seldom considered and yet are vital to unlocking our potential. Without addressing them, many people would never be able to achieve what they want in life, despite dealing with their negative beliefs and current-life emotional baggage.

I also decided to attempt to build up a chronological existence timeline for myself. By reading my biofield, I started to receive the data that gradually revealed the history of my existence. The information that I received confirmed many incarnations. I was able to access the data relating to which region of the world I had lived in, my gender, social status and my main life lessons. I also had information about how I had died during these past lives and how I had made soul contracts, the energy of which carried forward into this lifetime.

I had some astonishing revelations about the effect of my past incarnations on my current life choices. The clarity I gained helped me in many ways – and it changed the way I view life. Through my experiences and subsequent work with my clients, I now know that past-life experiences are very important for us to recognise. The disturbance of past-life traumas can influence our current life choices and relationships. In fact, a whole other level of connections, recognitions and embedded energetic patterns exist in what I term our soul heritage. You will find out what they are in Part Three of this book. First, though, let's turn our attention to Relationship Energy Principles in Part Two.

Part Two: **What Lies Between Us**

Several years ago, a young woman was working in an office. She went in as usual every day. The work was all right, but she noticed that the atmosphere was not great; it was always tense. People kept themselves to themselves. Nobody reached out to chat. It meant that the quality of life at work was not enjoyable. She became used to it. That was just the way things were. It was accepted and not questioned by anybody.

One day, when she came into the office, she noticed that something was different. A group of people were chatting in an animated way around the coffee machine. During the day, colleagues came out from behind their computers and communicated with their co-workers. Somehow the atmosphere had a lighter quality to it; something like a mental sigh of relief permeated the place. She even heard the sound of laughter for the first time since she had been there.

She went home that night feeling better than ever before. She slept better. Next day, the same thing happened. For a whole two weeks, her experience at work was great. She made new friends with some co-workers who had started chatting with her and everything seemed so much easier. Secretly, she had been looking for another job, but it didn't seem so urgent now.

Then, one day, she went into the office and her throat tightened. She felt it immediately. The tension was back. Nobody was talking and the mood was subdued. As she sat at her desk, all day long she kept on wondering what had changed. She went home that night and carried on pondering the question. She didn't sleep well.

Next day, as she entered the building, she was overcome by the same feeling of tension and when she entered the office it was clear that everyone else felt it too. She was perplexed. No one had left, no one had joined. The boss seemed the same. There had been no bad news given to the company.

As she thought about it further, she realised that there was only one factor that had changed and coincided with the timing. One co-worker had been off on holiday for the previous two weeks and had returned to work the day before. That was when the mood changed. She was negative, constantly complained and made everything difficult for others. The young woman realised that the co-worker's mere presence was enough to completely affect the mood of the building. Her colleague was broadcasting unhappiness.

The young woman was called Sigal Barsade and she went on to base her career on what she had observed. She became a professor at the Wharton School in the University of Pennsylvania. She called her discovery 'emotional contagion'.

Because I work with energy, her findings make perfect sense to me. Emotions are not just due to brain chemistry and hormonal response, they have vibrational frequencies. We are all constantly broadcasting the truth of how we feel. Just as dogs sense our fear, other people consciously and unconsciously react to our true feelings, however much we try to hide them.

I want to draw your attention back to what you now know about the biofield. What laws of energy does it subscribe to? Remember the characteristics that we discussed at the start of Part One: The Vibrational Human. But how does this underpin and influence our tangible reality? How do we see these energetic laws determining how a relationship develops with someone? The energetic world sometimes seemingly goes against all logic. However, as you are also made of energy, then all of these laws apply to you as well. So let's look at what this means for you as a human:

➤ Energetically you are billions of years old!

➤ You are linked vibrationally to everyone and everything in your environment. You do not live in isolation: just by living you affect everything.

➤ You are able to change your internal state and what you transmit by changing the form your energy takes.

➤ The impact and imprint of everything you have experienced remain as energetic information within your biofield.

It becomes evident that what Sigal Barsade discovered is not so surprising. We have to look at ourselves and our environment in a context that is beyond accepted reasoning.

The stark fact is that the quality of your relationships with others is highly influenced by what you are transmitting energetically. So from a vibrational point of view, I want to shed light on what happens when we interact with another person's biofield.

Your biofield is reacting to your thoughts, emotions and actions all of the time. A healthy human biofield extends at least 4 metres (13 feet) out from the physical body. Yours is consciously awake and responsive to your environment. When you enter a room, you take your biofield and all that it contains with you; so if you tell people you are happy and you are not, they will energetically know the truth even if their mind persuades them otherwise. This can cause confusion and mixed messages, because we have been taught that the mind is the dominant factor in human intelligence, so it is easy to be convinced by it and override our deep energetic knowing.

Furthermore, when someone else is carrying an emotion that you hold as well, your state will be influenced either positively or negatively by them. This is why we talk about an electrifying presence. It can be almost impossible to stay unaffected by others in this situation, as energetically you have little idea how dramatically you are responding. You can get triggered by your own unresolved emotional states and disempowering thought-patterns and beliefs, often on an unconscious level. This is why a whole building can be affected by one person's negative thoughts and feelings.

Now that I have set the scene, I want to share something with you that will change your perceptions. There is an effect that is well known by musicians and it holds true for emotional states too.

111

Sympathetic Resonance

This is a phenomenon which can be experienced with tuning forks. If you place two tuning forks with the same pitch next to each other and you sound one of them, the other will start vibrating all by itself. This is called 'sympathetic resonance'. Like a musical tone, emotions carry a vibration of their own, which means that they are affected by sympathetic resonance too. Specific emotions have a specific wavelength, so if you are vibrating with anger, another person who is also vibrating with anger can increase your own levels. This is why we can witness a sudden escalation of violence in many tragic situations. However, if you let go of negative emotions and broadcast positive feelings, others will increase the levels of their positive emotion too.

When you change your emotional state, you change your energy transmission – and you will be amazed at how differently people react to you. I have worked with people who went from being ignored by everyone in their office, to being the most popular person whom everyone wanted to talk to. The change took place because they let go of issues such as their anxiety about other people liking them, or their anger at something that happened in the past. Resolving negative emotions is the most powerful way of changing how others treat you.

Separator and Connector Emotions

Our emotions can be put into two categories: those that enable us to empathise with others and those that isolate us from others. On the most fundamental level, there is only one real separator emotion and that is fear. All other separator emotions are just various aspects of how fear manifests in our lives. For example, anger is the reaction to a fear of loss of control over a situation, while guilt is the fear of having done something to jeopardise our physical security because of being blamed and ostracised by others. On the other hand, the fundamental connector emotion is love and all other connector emotions are aspects of this.

Emotions have a resonance that forms a spectrum of wave frequencies, just like light and sound. I have shared the following table (opposite) to illustrate how each of the 13 vortices of

Vortex of Light	Connector Emotion	Separator Emotion	Positive Mental State	Negative Mental State
Earth	Assurance	Insecurity, vulnerability	Grounded	Indecision and being in limbo
Root	Stability	Anger	Group safety	Lack of belonging
Sacral	Confidence	Disempowerment, helplessness	Capability	Worthlessness
Solar Plexus	Calm	Fear, anxiety	Self-care	Hypervigilance
Heart	Love, gratitude	Grief, jealousy	Commitment	Distrust
Universal Heart	Compassion, empathy	Compassion fatigue, heartlessness	Unconditional care of others	Being put upon and unappreciated
Transcendental Heart	Joy	Jadedness	Success and fulfilment	Disappointed with the outcome
Throat	Creativity	Feeling stifled	Expressiveness	Unheard, unseen, unappreciated
Third eye	Inspiration	Confusion	Self-evaluation	Procrastination
Cosmic Third Eye	Elation	Hopelessness	Ability to see the larger picture	Scepticism about the possibility of happiness
Crown	Certainty	Feeling lost	Humanitarianism	Judging others
Halo	Peacefulness	Doubt	Ability to trust unseen guidance	Inability to trust life
Soul Star	Liberation	Despair	At oneness, equilibrium and expanded consciousness	Feeling disconnected from others

How the 13 vortices of light can help you

light (see the introduction to Part One, pages 50–53) resonate with a range of emotions in that spectrum. I have also listed the positive and negative mental states that go with each emotion. It is sometimes difficult to separate what you are feeling from what you are thinking and hopefully this will give you clarity. Emotions are a reaction triggered by our thoughts. Revisit the chapter 'Mind Traps and Bright Choices' and reread the information about the Survival Calculation to refresh your understanding of how that works.

How the 13 Vortices of Light Affect the Way We See the World

When I work with my clients, I always start a Life Retuning session by checking their fundamental energy anatomy – and that includes the 13 vortices of light. I want to make sure that there is an uninterrupted current of energy flowing through all of them. To me, this sets the foundations for living successfully.

During the years that I have been running my private biofield psychology practice, I've discovered something incredible. As you know, colours are not solid: they are electromagnetic vibrations. That means that when we look at a colour, our eyes are interpreting it and translating it to our brain. But I discovered that the state of our thinking and our emotional wellbeing affects the way we see colours too.

Every colour has a purity point, where it is neither too bright nor too dull. Knowing this, I use a set of special colour cards to check the colour perception of my clients. There is a matching colour card for each of the vortices of light and I invite the client to choose which cards they perceive to be too dull and which ones as being too bright. I then check each of the corresponding energy centres and diagnose whether they are balanced and open or unbalanced and locked in the client.

Having worked with over 1000 people all over the world, I have found an eye-opening correlation: two people can see the same colour completely differently. For example, one person may see a red card as dull while another finds it too vibrant, suggesting that the root vortex is highly likely to be out of balance or even locked in these individuals. On checking, 99.9 per cent of the time, this is correct. But that is not where the revelation ends. When I apply my Life Retuning techniques and ascertain that the vortex is now balanced and open, the same two people will report that the red card now looks 'normal'. Today, when I use the test on all of the vortices of light in a client's energy anatomy, I already know what the state of their vortices will be, based on how the client perceives the associated colour cards.

So what sends our vortices of light out of balance and causes them to shut down? I have found that unresolved distressing emotions are the number 1 cause. High emotion can overload our system and blow an electromagnetic fuse in our biofield. The vortices act as a control mechanism, preventing that overload from happening. If we do not resolve those emotions and keep being triggered by them, certain energy centres can remain locked for many years, and other people can be the trigger for this because of sympathetic resonance.

Your energy anatomy provides a road map to self-diagnosis. Pay attention to how you are responding to colours and you can very quickly identify any hidden emotions or patterns of thinking that you need to be aware of.

The Eyes Have It

Some fascinating research has been done recently which underpins how powerfully we affect each other. Have you ever been in a situation where you have felt that someone was staring at you? Even if your back was turned, you just knew that their eyes were on you. Nothing happened physically, no one said anything, but you just knew that you were being observed.

Rupert Sheldrake PhD is a renowned biologist and biochemist who became fascinated by the curious feeling many of us possess when we are stared at from behind He has conducted many experiments using a simple procedure. The testee sits with their back to the tester. The tester either looks at them or looks away and the testee notes down what they think is happening. Volunteers around the globe took part in this research and Sheldrake found a significant effect. The results showed that 427 people were more often right than wrong in detecting what was happening, as opposed to 157 who were more wrong than right. He concludes that 'the results suggest that the feeling of being looked at from behind is a real phenomenon that depends on factors as yet unknown to science.'

The biofield could provide a likely answer for this phenomenon. When a person feels the electromagnetic focused attention emanating from someone else's energy anatomy, this would cause an energetic reaction which they would sense on some indefinable level. This would probably make them feel uncomfortable.

Sheldrake postulates that the phenomenon of being looked at from behind 'may be of evolutionary significance in the relationships between predators and prey'. Our caveman and cavewoman ancestors are likely to have had a heightened sense of awareness of their environment, including when they were being sized up for lunch by a wild animal! I am sure it made a vital difference many times.

So you can now appreciate why what you are transmitting to others makes the difference in the quality of relationships you allow yourself to have.

Relationship Energy Principle 11

If you feel the disharmonious energy of someone, look inside yourself to find the same vibration and bring it to your conscious awareness.

I have mentioned how the phenomenon of sympathetic resonance carries through to our thoughts and our emotions. You can take advantage of this knowledge in a very empowering way when it comes to your relationships. It is actually a natural and simple gift that you can use to your benefit.

Like Reflects Like

You may have heard of the saying 'like attracts like'; well, it is not just an old wives' tale, it's describing sympathetic resonance (see page 112). On the basis of this, I am going to share a super tip that you can use to help yourself.

First, I'd like you to start noticing what kind of problems, emotional states and attitudes the people around you have. Is there a pattern?

Here is where you can empower yourself, because these people are showing you what is within yourself that is ready for you to bring to your awareness and release. Recognise the Mirror is a powerful exercise that you can use when you feel that there is something off-key with a relationship. You won't need to analyse anything, just act on what you read from what you are attracting in. When something is ready to change, it happens easily.

Recognise the Mirror

Sympathetic resonance provides you with a vibrational mirror. In light of this, make it a habit to ask yourself the following five questions to uncover your reflection if you find you are being negatively triggered by someone else:

➤ What is the emotion this person triggers in me?

➤ What is the number 1 belief or judgement I hold about this person?

➤ Does this person's behaviour remind me of anyone else I have had issues with in my life?

➤ Does this person do anything that I have not given myself permission to do?

➤ What is left to resolve within me?

This is such a beautiful and enlightening way of working on yourself. There is even a synergistic healing taking place between you and the other person. Einstein called it 'spooky action at a distance' and you will find out shortly how incredible this behaviour of energy is.

This way of harnessing your energy cleans your system every day, leaving you excited, positive yet calm and having total awareness of how to resolve any issue, no matter what it is. When you can do that, you notice that the kind of people you attract into your life enriches the quality of your relationships.

By doing the Recognise the Mirror exercise, you will discover that everyone in your life reflects back to you what you are transmitting. Turn it into a clearing practice for yourself and you will create harmony, healing and expansion for both yourself and others. This will lead to powerful transformations.

Relationship Energy Principle 12

Both happiness and unhappiness are habits. You need to
undo the habit of unhappiness first, before you can take
on the habit of happiness.

Happiness is the endless search for so many of us. If you
are in the disappointing outcome cycle, then your levels
of happiness and life satisfaction will struggle to rise.
There are many factors that contribute to how happy you are.
The standard indicators are based on how wealthy you are, how
healthy and whether you are single or in a relationship. But I
have discovered through my work that there is a key factor which
overrides these – and it is more to do with the social 'climate' of
happiness and the habit of unhappiness.

The Habit of Unhappiness

One of the most important parts of the work I do with my
clients is to reverse any self-limiting beliefs they hold. It is vital
to clear these to have any chance of achieving our desired goals
of good health, abundance, great relationships, fulfilment and...
happiness. The beliefs we hold create our reality. How we see
ourselves, others and the world depends on what is going on in
our minds. The level of our ability to achieve, survive and thrive
is set even before we act physically. A shockingly common belief
I have found to occur many times in the minds of people I worked
with is: 'Bad endings are a safe outcome.'

This got me asking the question, 'Why?' What led us to
hold this belief? Our minds create beliefs based on our previous
experiences. As you know, our minds perform the Survival
Calculation to keep us safe from perceived threats to our survival.

So if our minds see a bad ending as a safe outcome, it follows that the threat must come from a good outcome. But why should that be? The more I thought about it, the more I realised that our whole lives are set up for disasters.

The Unhappiness Sandwich

Day after day, what do we see on the internet news, the television, or hear about on the popular broadcasting channels? Accounts of disasters, trauma and horror. The media grooms us to expect despair, helplessness, anger, doom and fear.

Are you aware of how many years this has been going on? News has become Bad News. Journalists call any story with a happy outcome 'soft news'. For them, its purpose is to lighten the mood at the end of a news broadcast after all of the doom-and-gloom bulletins.

On the other hand, our social media has been built on showcasing people who have perfect bodies and look to be living perfect lives. The gap between illusion and reality has recently widened, as companies are now using digital 'models' like Shudu Gram, which are made up of pixels – yet have millions of followers. They are moving further and further away from reality into an unattainable fantasy world. As an up-and-coming digital model agency attests, 'There is nothing comparable!' They are right: totally unattainable non-human perfection has arrived. And I predict that unhappiness levels will rise even higher.

In 2002, a film called *S1mOne* was released, starring Al Pacino. The story is about a film producer who creates a digital actress that everyone thinks is real. A bunch of pixels becomes an overnight success. It was a science fiction film at the time, and in the story, people think S1mOne is a real person and they became completely obsessed with finding out more about its life. The thing is, it doesn't have a life. Now here it is: science fiction has become fact.

More and more studies are revealing how damaging social media has already become. Upping the ante and creating more illusions that look real, companies are focusing our attention more strongly on what we are lacking and craving in our lives.

As fantasy and reality merge, our minds will find it harder and harder to distinguish between the two.

The same digital model agency as mentioned earlier writes in its promotional material: 'It makes little difference to people if the star on Instagram is "real". What is "real" on Instagram?' I disagree. Real means real life and the experiences we have of real life; unreal means a fantasy that is not a real experience and, often, can never be. Real people live real lives; pixels don't.

The danger is that our mind makes no distinction between the imagined and the real. The same areas of the brain are activated. In 2014, a researcher called Brian Clark conducted an experiment at Ohio University on a set of healthy individuals to see whether an exercise using the imagination could affect our muscles. The volunteers had their wrists wrapped in a cast for four weeks. During that time, they were asked to imagine strong muscle contractions for 11 minutes a day without moving any muscles. The results showed how entwined our minds are with our bodies: at the end of the four weeks, the volunteers' muscle strength was measured against a control group who had not done any visualisation exercises. Those who had done the exercise in their imaginations had twice as strong muscles as the control group.

Imagine how your mind is influenced by both the news and social media. Programmed to feel anxious and helpless on the one hand, and to be lacking and craving the unattainable on the other. You are trapped in between the two: the news of doom and gloom and the fake perfection of social media. You are in the Unhappiness Sandwich.

It Takes Courage To Be Happy!

It may seem a strange thing to say that it takes courage to be happy, but it's true. The Unhappiness Sandwich keeps us oscillating between negative feelings. In fact, happiness is the stranger sitting opposite you. The reason it takes courage to be happy is because we are so used to life being a challenge and we have been taught that it will always have to be that way. But the truth is that we create our own reality: what we believe is what we perceive, achieve and receive.

It is entirely up to us personally whether we live an unhappy life or are brave enough to try out happiness. It is totally our own responsibility. We have all been in the wars and suffered disappointments, disaster, harshness, exploitation or relationship pain and gone through the fallout of these experiences. Nobody escapes because we are here to learn the deeper wisdom inherent in the human condition. When we experience these hard times, we tend to behave reactively. We suffer from anxiety, doubt, depression, anger and all the other distressing emotions that we can feel as human beings. We may even become physically ill and have pain in our bodies. But the one thing that knits all of our reactive behaviours together is that they are familiar. Our society makes it the done thing to strive for happiness and wellbeing, yet at the same time, we are actually expected to be unhappy and unwell. That's how so many pills get to be sold and dieting products have become a multi-billion dollar industry. We put ourselves under pressure to change ourselves, because we are constantly being told that we are not good enough and that we do not possess enough.

Then there is the way we value people in society. Material possessions and financial wealth have been seen as the confirmation of a successful and happy life for a very long time. The feudal system was based on this. The rich had everything and the poor were serfs who answered their every need. People were there to be exploited, whatever they had to offer – their bodies, skills, knowledge, lives and deaths. Over the centuries, the majority of people have experienced unfair lives, inequality, pain, disappointment and suffering. You just have to watch any history programme to see it laid out in searing detail. What a sad tale to tell when there is such a potential for a very different quality of life.

Our shared history means that we are programmed to expect disaster. Bad outcomes are the 'devils we know', so how much scarier is it to contemplate an emotion that most of us experience as fleeting... happiness? Many influencers talk about how to use the Law of Attraction to turn our lives around and suddenly become satisfied, peaceful and... happy. But if we don't address the reality of what we have inherited from the past and undo the habit of unhappiness, then it remains a struggle to become happy.

The fact is that most people have no idea how to start changing their happiness levels.

The mind views happiness as an unknown quantity – a new territory – and that is scary. It views happiness as being a threat to our survival, even though this seems crazy. Anything it views as a threat, it will do its utmost to stop us from experiencing. That is why this belief – about the risk presented by happiness – exists in so many minds.

The Happiness Frontier

By accepting happiness, we are stepping into unknown territory. What might happen if a challenging situation arises and, instead of getting angry or upset, we were to choose to go inside ourselves and see the blessing and lesson that this experience is showing to us? That takes courage. It takes courage to open yourself up to the possibility that life does not have to be a struggle. It is much easier to expect the struggle, 'the devil you know', even if it keeps you unhappy, because it is the known.

So let's look at the scenario that takes place when we think about the possibility of being permanently happy. Here are a few of the sort of thoughts that might be going through our minds:

➤ OK, so I am happy, this feels good – but what happens now?

➤ Can I cope with smiling all of the time?

➤ How long can this state last?

➤ Isn't it inevitable that I will feel unhappy again?

➤ How do I respond to someone else telling me about their pain if I am feeling happy?

➤ Will other people accept me being happy all of the time or will I be judged and seen as weird?

➤ Will they think me unsympathetic to the perceived state the world is in?

➤ Do I need distressing emotions such as anxiety, fear and anger anymore?

You see, in order to take on the habit of happiness, we have to create a whole new set of responses, mentally, emotionally and physically. And we are simply not used to it. There is so much we need to change about the choices we make in reaction to life.

In my work, I often find that my clients in Australia, the UK, USA, Saudi Arabia and various other countries are experiencing the same thought patterns, beliefs, emotional states and even physical complaints on the same day. This goes cross-culture, cross-sex, cross-age, cross-distance. There is a collective link with these themes. We have to start taking this seriously. The more people can be successfully happy, the easier it will be for everyone else. Because the happiness vibration will be changing the collective consciousness state across the planet.

It is time to rewrite your relationship with happiness and ensure that you have great outcomes.

Uncovering Your Logical Happiness Limiters

Use your inner Yes/No to work through the next exercise.

➤ First, go back to 'How to Get to Know Your Inner Yes/ No' on page 63 and remind yourself of the process and the checks.

➤ Now, say the following out loud: 'Bad endings are a safe outcome.' Does it fit with you on some deep level, do you feel any resistance against it – or does it just sound like words? Without allowing your mind to jump in and tell you this is rubbish, sit with your responses and make a note of how your energy reacts.

➤ There are three significant beliefs that you need to check next. They will help you to build up your happiness muscle and to develop the habit of happiness. Say each of the following out loud:

➤ It is safe for me to be happy.

➤ I deserve to be happy.

➤ I give myself permission to be happy.

➤ What does your inner Yes/No tell you about what is true for you each time?

➤ Have a go at the sway test (see 'How to Do the Biofield Sway', page 65) and discover what happens to your body when you repeat these three statements.

Start to observe where a negative belief about happiness is playing out in your life. Notice your patterns of thinking and once you know what triggers those thoughts, make a choice to respond in a determinedly different way, a happy way. Either do this instinctively or plan how you want to respond and do that instead. Write down a list of your planned responses. Smile. Take some slow, deep breaths...

What is the positive within the negative? Consciously find it and focus on it.

The more you do this, the more your mental pathways will adjust. Neutrons that fire together, wire together. This is called neuroplasticity. Our minds are very malleable if we have the right tools to work with them.

The next time you watch the news, see if you can pick out the drama archetypes and notice how you respond to them. It is an eye-opening experience to see what is happening to you outside of the content of the stories. What thoughts and emotions do they trigger in you?

Let's supercharge your happiness levels so you are on track to develop the habit of happiness.

Relationship Energy Principle 13

Do not give your energy away to others through the
vehicles of need, obligation, denial, blame or addiction.

Your personal energy is so important. It is your life force. It
is your bubbling source of action and positivity. Imagine a
bottle of champagne. Before you take the cork out, it is full
of bubbles and effervescence. If you take the cork out and leave
it on the side, the fizz eventually goes and you end up with flat
champagne. You let the bubbles escape somewhere else, leaving
you with a dull drink. We are like that champagne bottle, full
of fizz until we let others take it away and we become flat and
depleted of energy. There are several ways we give our energy
away or allow others to take it.

Need

We can become needy when we do not feel we can provide or
generate what we require internally. That is when we look outside
of ourselves for fulfilment. This false fulfilment can take the form
of substances, environments, behaviours or other people. As
soon as we focus our search for fulfilment outside ourselves, we
lose perspective of ourselves. We no longer progress our internal
development, but may instead distort the true value of whatever it
is that we are investing our interest in on the outside. We can fall
into the trap of devaluing ourselves and elevating whatever it is
that we are hooking in to. This can lead to feelings of depression,
inadequacy and helplessness. We have given our power away.

We need to start recognising our own worth and that we
already have access to everything we need within ourselves. As
soon as we start to feel into our own value, we have brought

back the power to make the changes we want. By transmitting the frequency of our own worth, we will attract those situations and people who will confirm it to us.

Obligation

Many of us have been brought up to think that there are people, organisations, causes or affiliations that we must be obligated to. No matter what, we are expected to subsume our own needs and put others first. Let me explain why this is a set-up that can lead to disaster for us. By putting another first, we can starve ourselves of the nourishment we need in our own lives. This can lead to the state of sacrifice. How much are we willing to sacrifice to make someone else happy?

The problem with this is that not only do we end up depleted of our own life energy, but we also contort ourselves in ways which are not truthful. If we are not living our truth, eventually we will end up in either emotional, mental or physical pain. We have given our power away and we cannot look after our own needs.

Examine whether what or who you feel obligated to is really aligned with your own journey and, if not, then consider letting it go. Recognise your own deeper truth.

Denial

Denial comes with a stubbornness to see the reality of a situation. We can hang on to something or someone for far too long after it is no longer serving us. Deep down inside, we know that things are not working, but we are so scared to look at the truth that we stay in a state of denial. We also tend to push away anyone who tries to get us to look at the reality of the situation.

By refusing to see the truth, we have disempowered ourselves of the means to make a situation better and healthier. The longer we insist on being in denial, the more acute the wrongness of the situation often becomes. Eventually, something has to give – and we often end up hurt when things finally explode before our eyes and we can no longer ignore them. This outcome can lead to feelings of distrust, uncertainness and anger, which leads on to the next way in which we can give our power away, which is blame.

Examine what is and is not serving you in your life. If you feel a resistance to that examination around any issue, ask yourself why you are so scared to look at it. By answering this question honestly and dealing with it, you can take your power back and move out of the stuck state.

Blame

When things go wrong in our lives, we can feel angry and resentful. This anger and resentment often lead us to blame another, as we are unable to accept responsibility for what we have allowed to happen or even created. We can be frightened to address our fears of not being good enough, lovable enough, smart enough, capable enough. We do not want to engage with thoughts that might otherwise lead us to acknowledge we believe we really are stupid, worthless, unlovable or useless. The only other option is to put the blame outside of ourselves. Once we have done this, we can feel righteous indignation and indulge fully in feeling hurt.

The next logical step is to forget the truth of what actually happened and rewrite history in our heads. We end up believing that false history and hold on to the feelings of blame. Our energy feeds our hurt feelings – and this can last for years and lead to us holding on to grudges. The truth is that we have given away our power.

If you recognise this, re-examine the original situation and accept the truth in a courageous way. Accept responsibility for your part in creating it and then forgive yourself for all of the hurt you've caused yourself and the love you've denied yourself because of it.

Addiction

I have talked about neediness being a major way in which we give away our power, and how we can devalue ourselves as part of this process. I want to address the other side of this equation. When we have created a life which is full of trauma, anxiety, anger, fear or depression, we want to escape from the emotional pain. We must find a way to numb it all out. This is when we are in danger of becoming addicted to something or someone.

If we are battling with distress and unhappiness, we are often investing a lot of energy in just coping on a day-to-day basis. This leaves us weak and vulnerable. Whatever we are addicted to will end up controlling us and can rule our lives. Every decision we make can end up being based on whether we can get our next fix or not. We will come up with logically clever excuses for why we are hooked in. We allow our minds to play tricks, give us false information and create illusions any time we decide to try to break free. Our hearts cry out that something is wrong with this situation, but our minds drown out that truthful voice.

There is only one way to break free and that is to courageously address the distress which has built up. Be aware that your mind will do everything it can to stop you from focusing on it. It will see your attempt as a threat to the logical protection it has built around the core issue.

Later on in this book, I will be giving you an Energy Aware tool that will help you to transform upsetting feelings without triggering your mind directly.

Relationship Energy Principle 14

Unchain yourself from resentment and forgive yourself and others for the past. See yourself and others through the eyes of compassion and empathy.

One of the hardest things we struggle with as human beings is the ability to forgive others for the harm we perceive they have done to us. We wrestle with feelings of anger, resentment, disappointment, injustice, rejection and fear. When we cannot let go of these feelings concerning another person, our consciousness is held in the past instead of allowing us to live in the present moment. When we cannot forgive another, we are denying ourselves a route out of emotional pain. Sometimes, we may behave in ways that are calculated to punish them but even this ultimately only ends up hurting us, because we are cutting ourselves off from the possibility of healing the relationship or moving on from it. If we put our energy into blaming someone else, we also fail to recognise the parts that we have played in creating or allowing the situation to occur. The danger here is that we are likely to end up in a similar situation again.

We can collect grudges and hurts until there is no room left in our hearts for any love. But if we can let go of blame and resentment, we instantly free ourselves up from negative energy. We also need to forgive ourselves for our part in creating these situations in the first place. By being unforgiving towards ourselves, we attract punishment, which will show up in our lives either emotionally, mentally or physically. In order to keep ourselves healthy and loving, we must let go of all and forgive all. On an energetic level, this also changes the person we were holding negative feelings towards. We are all energetically linked and we affect each other, even if we are not physically in the same place.

Untying the Knot

In Greek, one word for forgiveness is *aphienai*, which has its roots in a term that means untying a knot. Energetically, a lack of forgiveness interrupts the connection of heart-centred energy; it is like going on hunger strike. Forgiveness is about a freeing up and a reestablishment of that connection.

A lack of forgiveness and resentment is an energetic poison that can affect everything. If you do not alter it, you can end up holding a cynical perspective and a feeling of resentment against the world. This is a very toxic way to live. It is like punching yourself and expecting the person you are angry at to feel your pain.

The healthy way of finding the route into forgiveness is by practising atonement. If you separate the word atonement out into parts, it becomes 'at-one-ment' – of becoming whole again. Forgiveness is the greatest gift that you can give yourself and the greatest wisdom you can apply when it comes to other people in your life.

Forgiveness does not mean you condone someone else's behaviour. It simply means that you have let go of the hurt it caused you and released them from it too.

When you feel you have been mistreated, it is natural to feel angry and resentful. It's hard to forgive. It's hard to let go of those feelings. But the truth is that when you can't forgive, you don't get over your wounds and instead you bond yourself to that person with a binding that is more powerful than steel. This is because when you won't let them go, they will continue to restrict your level of happiness.

Forgiveness does not mean that you are excusing what has happened to you. Forgiving does not mean that you give up your power. In fact it is exactly the opposite. When you forgive someone, you take back your power from them. You release them and yourself at the same time.

The Forgiveness Prayer

The Polynesians have known the deep healing wisdom of forgiveness for many years. They practise Ho'oponopono. I am honoured to have a very close friend who is an indigenous healer of Samoan descent. One day we were discussing the topic of forgiveness and she told me the story of how Ho'oponopono came about in the Polynesian islands.

Long, long ago, the people of the islands fought amongst themselves, brother against brother and family against family. There was a huge and tragic loss of life. People couldn't escape from the violence because they were trapped on the individual islands. The situation became so bad that the elders decided to come together to find a solution to stop the tragedies. They understood the power of forgiveness, so they instituted a ritual which included the Ho'oponopono forgiveness prayer. My friend explained that from that time onwards, the tribes would regularly come together and perform a collective release of feelings of blame, resentment and anger. This was a time where each member of the tribal family would actively and intentionally forgive all of the members for anything that they felt had hurt them or injured them.

As a result, a miraculous change took place across the Polynesian islands: violence levels dropped and harmony increased in the relationships that people had on every level. The wisdom of the Polynesian elders had made the difference and revealed how powerful the energy of forgiveness is in healing feuds, grudges and hatred.

After talking with my friend, I created my own version of the Ho'oponopono prayer. I find it to be a very powerful way to cleanse negative energy and raise the vibration levels. I routinely say it several times whenever I go for a walk on the beach. You can use it too:

Divine Creator,
Father, Mother, Daughter, Son as One,
If I, my family, relatives and ancestors,
Have offended your family, relatives and ancestors
In thought, word, deed and action,

From the beginning of time,
Until this present moment,
We ask forgiveness.
Let this cleanse, release and purify
All negative emotions, blocks, and vibrations,
And let all negative, unwanted energies
Be transmuted into healing light.

One day, I was talking with my ex-partner when it led to a very important conversation. He had just watched a news story about a tragedy in which lives were lost. He astonished me by saying, 'I wish that I had more compassion.' He had realised that his feelings did not match with the level of the tragedy. He felt a disconnection and could not empathise. This conversation raised several questions with me which I want to share with you, because they can help you to measure your own compassion levels.

A Question of Compassion

How do you know that you either have or do not have enough compassion?

➤ If you do not feel you have enough compassion, what is it that makes you think you need to have more?

➤ Who do you consider as having enough compassion?

➤ How do you measure compassion?

➤ What would you do to change the situation?

After Forgiveness, Compassion Can Come

'A human being is a part of the whole called by us
"Universe," a part limited in time and space. He
experiences himself, his thoughts and feelings as
something separated from the rest – a kind of optical
delusion of his consciousness. This delusion is a kind of
prison for us, restricting us to our personal desires and to
affection for a few persons nearest to us. Our task must be
to free ourselves from this prison by widening our circle of
compassion to embrace all living creatures and the whole
of nature in its beauty.'
– Albert Einstein, theoretical physicist

While we are focusing on blame, we cannot feel
compassion. In fact, revengefulness can result from
focusing on blame. Revenge is a blindfold that shuts
us off from the reality of a situation. When it comes to making
decisions, this is a disaster waiting to happen. Never make a
decision from a position of no forgiveness, because your intention
carries the essence of that action into the outcome. Instead, work
on releasing the feeling as soon as possible.

When blame and revenge have been replaced by the feeling of
compassion, this is the time to make a decision. Whereas blame
is a separator emotion, compassion is a connector. Compassion
is a form of love that recognises and empathises with others. It is
when our hearts go out to others. It brings our heads up out of
our own problems, to be able to see the whole picture. It is when
we feel oneness with every living being. We wish for them to stop
hurting, to be happy and healthy.

Compassion is capable of creating miracles – and you are the
person in control of activating it in your life. Compassion even
changes the way our brains function. We become One on another
level, vibrationally our brainwaves synchronise and a different
part of our brains switches on.

In 2008, a discovery was made that led to an illuminating
study. The Dalai Lama sent some senior Tibetan monks to work
with a researcher at the University of Wisconsin. Using fMRI
scans, Richard Davidson was studying the effect of compassion

meditation on the brain. What he found out when he scanned the brains of the monks amazed him and led him to do further research. The monks were masters at generating feelings of loving–kindness and compassion. Their brain scans showed that their left frontal lobe was unusually highly activated. This is the part of our brains that is associated with our ability to feel empathy, whereas the right frontal lobe is prominent in feelings of negative emotions.

Davidson continued his research with some more volunteers, including 16 Tibetan monks and an age-matched control group. These monks had completed at least 10,000 hours of compassionate meditation. This is the standard level the Tibetan monks attain. They taught the other volunteers how to go through a routine of compassion meditation – and the results showed that even with this little training, the volunteers' brains were already activating the left frontal lobe.

This means that the answer to my ex-partner's wish is that it is possible to increase our levels of compassion. The best way I have found to increase our feelings of compassion apart from meditation is RAAK.

RAAK

RAAK stands for 'random acts of anonymous kindness'. It is a powerful way to activate your heart energy, and takes the practice of random acts of kindness one step further. By acting anonymously, your ego mind does not get the reward of someone saying, 'Thank you.'

It may feel uncomfortable at the beginning, but if you persevere with this practice, you will find that your heart energy will become amplified and it will help to free you up from any expectations you have of others. It is when we have an expectation of another person and they let us down which leads to blame, grudges and an absence of forgiveness. RAAK can help you to break free of this pattern.

Relationship Energy Principle 15

Give gratitude for what you have and learn to hold a joyful anticipation for what has not yet shown up in your life.

One of the most powerful energies of intention we can hold is that of gratitude. It is a transformational action. It is not a wishy-washy notion that can be done in a half-hearted way. As you know, there is scientific research showing that emotions and thoughts hold their own signature energy frequencies. We now know that love and appreciation create a state of coherence in our systems, which in turn supports emotional stability, mental clarity and better health. All this from saying 'thank you' and truly meaning it!

The Power of Gratitude

In order to be able to be grateful, we need to let go of any resentment towards ourselves and others. We need to make a commitment to transcend any feelings of blame and judgement and denial. Remember the canal boat which cannot go forward until the water level is the same on both sides of the lock? So it is with negative feelings: they won't allow your vibrations to rise to match the energy frequency of gratitude.

Your inner power

Your inner power comes from the words that you speak to yourself in your mind – the story that you tell yourself about yourself. If you bathe your cells in negative commentary about yourself, others and the world, your system will reflect this internally as unhappiness, dissatisfaction and possibly even in physical conditions. If you focus on using words of positive power about everything that you experience, your whole body will transform on the cellular level and you will benefit in profound ways. Gratitude can be a most effective means in achieving this ideal state.

Your outer power

Your outer power originates in the fact that energy has a vibrational frequency and, as you know, each thought that you have will be broadcast like radio waves into the world. The saying 'what goes around comes around' is ancient wisdom. The frequency of thoughts you transmit is the same frequency as whatever you attract in. You will get what you expect. So learn to use the energy of gratitude to unlock the real power of intention and throw a positive transformational pebble in the water, which will send those ripples throughout the world and into your life.

Having and Receiving

How good are you at receiving? You know about gratitude for what you already have, but how good are you at receiving what you do not yet have? Why don't people get what they want? Perhaps you have an idea about what you want to achieve in life and then it just doesn't seem to match up or quite correlate with how things turn out. You are working so hard to get what you want, but your hard work seems to be making little difference. That may be because you have not been using extended gratitude. Let me explain the difference between the gratitude I have already talked about and gratitude at a higher level.

Having

'Having' is when you have achieved the accumulation of something you wanted. That could be money, property, or that guy or girl who you wanted to share your life with. It could just be having a bit of peace and harmony. 'Having' is the moment where you are experiencing a tangible achievement. You can feel gratitude for what you know you have.

As a society, we have been learning how to become better

at the 'attitude of gratitude'. You may have listened to experts advising you to get up in the morning and consciously go through everything you are grateful for. This can include your friends, family, health, nature and the sun rising. This is beautiful energy and it is very important to have this state of the heart. Gratitude for what we have received creates a vibrational emanation and shapes our world.

The higher vibration of extended gratitude

I am going to tell you how you can raise your gratitude vibration to an even higher frequency. The intention to feel grateful for what we have received is one thing, but the intention to be grateful for what we do not yet have is quite another thing. Because it relies on something intangible and unseen. I call this 'extended gratitude'.

Extended gratitude is about having joyful anticipation that things will work out in the way you want them – yet without having any tangible proof that they will. It is a gratefulness for what will show up. Because when you are able to hold this higher level of gratitude, you are also sending out the higher vibrational frequency to attract it in. I find that the desired outcome tends to show up very quickly.

How to Practise Extended Gratitude

> ➤ Take the energy of all of your gratitude – and feel it swell your heart with a warm, loving energy.

> ➤ Breathe that energy in and feel your cells being bathed in it.

> ➤ Then focus that wonderful energy and send it out into the world.

Resistance

In general, we are not good at extended gratitude. It creates a different kind of energy emanation, because it is a different form of intention. When you want something to happen, you hope, you pray, you crave. You might even bargain with the Universe: 'If I can have this I promise I will do X, Y or Z' – but emotions of need and desperation may actually be blocking you from what you want, coming true. That is because the vibrational frequencies you are creating are of lack. So how can you be blocking the channel?

If you are holding resistance, you are stopping the manifestation from happening. This can show up in the following two ways: doubt and disappointment.

Doubt

The first way is when you don't believe that it is possible for what you want to happen. You have set a logical limiter on the potential outcome, which you may be unaware of. You may say that you believe it is possible. You may be saying affirmations every day about what you want. You may even stand in front of 1000 people and tell them you believe you will achieve what you want. But do you really believe it? When you use your inner Yes/No and allow yourself to know the truth, you will know the answer to that question. As you focus on an affirmation, if you don't truly believe it then you are actually focusing your mind on your disbelief instead, because the positive belief doesn't yet exist in your mind. It is the vibration of the disbelief that you are activating and it is likely that you will be disappointed with the outcome.

Disappointment

The other type of resistance you may be holding comes from having many experiences of being disappointed in the past, when you haven't achieved what you wanted. After a while, this erodes your ability to have positive expectations around something that hasn't happened as yet. However, through my work, I can tell you that it is energetically already in existence. There is an ancient maxim 'as above, so below'. You will find out in the Global Energy Principles section of this book why this is a universal truth. It means that the potential energy has already been created. But it has not yet shown up in the physical world. It is up to you to bring it into being. So it is possible that the reason you haven't received something is because you have blocked yourself off from the possibility of doing so.

Are you aware of a time when you know that you actually blocked yourself from receiving because you didn't believe enough in something coming true? Do you think your gratitude levels are up to the level you would like them to be? Perhaps you hope that they are, but you know that they are not.

Relationship Energy Principle 16

Honour others and cultivate an intention to listen to others as themselves, not through your own distorted view.

The dictionary definition of 'honour' is: to hold in great respect, hold in high esteem, have a high regard for. It may seem like an old-fashioned word in our Western culture, but not everywhere. In some parts of the world, the power of honouring is known and valued.

Have you ever known someone who does not acknowledge or value your experiences? When you tell them about your day, they don't ask you for any details about it. They don't show any interest or curiosity. They don't honour your feelings or your thoughts. Instead, they switch the conversation to their own experiences. They make it all about them.

If you are telling the story of something that happened to you which was unpleasant, they tell you that you should be grateful because other people are much worse off. Or they finish your sentences for you, assuming they know what you were going to say. They are negating your experiences and denying you the right to express yourself. Over the long-term, this can leave you with a belief that you have no right to acknowledge or validate your own life. Let's look at some examples of how differently people can behave.

The Neighbourhood That Gave the Best Christmas Gift

A while ago, I watched the most heart-warming video, which gave me a great swell of hope and joy. I'd started a Facebook group called Uplifting News. Uplifting News is a group where members can post real, uplifting news items to bring balance to what we read in the daily news, which has concentrated on sensationalist bad news stories for years. Members constantly share the most wonderful articles which put a lasting smile on their faces. Sometimes there is a story which affects me so much that I cannot do anything but sit in a state of wonder at how amazingly caring people can be, and this is one of these...

Imagine a whole neighbourhood learning to use sign language to surprise and delight a man who is deaf who lives among them? Imagine all of the local residents learning to sign in secret so that on a chosen day, no matter where he went, this man would be able to have a conversation with anyone in the area? This really happened in the suburb of Ba cılar in Istanbul, Turkey, and it is a wonderful example of understanding and honouring someone, making them feel that they matter and that they are special. Of being consciously present to the blessings and potential that others embody. Recognising the divine within them and generously mirroring back to them their worth. Holding sacred space for them to express their highest expression of themselves. Doing all of this without allowing their own egos to get in the way.

When we behave like this, miracles happen within our lives. We feel fulfilment on a deep level, which cannot be matched by any self-aggrandizement or self-serving act or material wealth. However, we can only get to that place when we are completely honest with ourselves about what is really going on in our lives. It is only when we are truly willing to see how we can change a situation, that we enable ourselves to make the change.

So it is with how we treat other people. As children, we learn from adults how to treat others – and if those adults did not honour others then they passed on those lessons. Do you think the current social media, news and most of the 'powers that be' demonstrate how to practise honouring? Yet these are the major influencers in our society and the teachers of our children now. The majority of them continue to perpetuate the 'treasure today, trash tomorrow' attitude that has got us into this state of mass loneliness, anxiety and depression.

Yet change is possible: to return to our Turkish story, a team from Samsung and an ad agency were responsible for the initiative that taught the neighbourhood sign language, which was part of a campaign to promote a new call centre for the deaf and hard-of-hearing in Turkey. So it goes to show that corporations can be forces for good, if they encourage kindness rather than division. Surely this must be an important part of the way forward for society as a whole?

How to Avoid Becoming an Emotional Hostage

It is very obvious to me how the quality of the treatment we received from adults affected us in both negative and positive ways when we were young. Certain teachers stand out as highly influential. Do you remember a teacher who altered your life? The encouragement I received from two particular teachers helped me to weave the threads of chemistry and history into my current interests and my work with Life Retuning. They gave me the gift of honouring my presence.

However, I also recall two teachers who caused me to lose my confidence because they did not know about honouring. One of them was a nun, which shocked me at the time. Through her behaviour towards me I developed a dislike of physics for a long time – until I discovered quantum physics and realised that it offers the route map for helping us to understand our lives. But I had to do my own inner work in order to get to that eureka insight. The other teacher saw me as a foreigner as she was still living in her colonial past where she had servants in India. To her, I was an inferior and her behaviour challenged me to investigate what I truly believed about myself.

When someone you look up to and admire holds a distorted view of themselves, they are seldom able to see you clearly. This can be a catalyst for disaster. There are two types of behaviour that can amplify your own feelings of vulnerability and put you at risk of becoming an emotional hostage. I call them 'buff 'n' puff' and 'link 'n' sink', and it is important that you avoid making choices whilst under the influence of their effects.

Buff 'n' Puff

Have you ever been in a situation where you were talking to someone and at the end of the conversation you felt like you were acting the part of a wad of Brasso that was being used to polish up the other person's ego? Did you feel respected, appreciated or heard? You might have found that apart from being asked a cursory 'How are you?' no other question came your way during the whole conversation. I call this Buff 'n' Puff. The other person is using you to buff themselves and then they puff up.

How did this encounter make you feel the rest of the day, the week, the month? Did you feel angry and rejected, doubting yourself and your worth? Did you feel used? A Buff 'n' Puffer can do a lot of psychological damage if you are vulnerable already and if your beliefs structures about yourself are shaky. Your presence isn't being honoured. In my experience and those of my clients, this behaviour happens a lot in the business environment.

Link 'n' Sink

Remember the Emotional Teddy Bears that I described in Personal Energy Principle 6? If you have not dealt with letting go of yours then you can become very vulnerable to this next type of behaviour from others. Those who Link 'n' Sink have got active passive-aggressive triggers and cannot tolerate those who seem to be happier and more fulfilled than they are. They have a need which makes them dangerous to your wellbeing. That need is to drag you down to the same level of unhappiness that they are feeling so that you are no longer causing them emotional pain with your happiness. Your happy state amplifies their unhappiness and they cannot stand it. So they will try to burst your bubble. They may drag you into their negative drama and then pull your energy and mood down with them, so that they can have you as a misery buddy and wallow in your shared company. They use you so that they can carry on with their dysfunctional behaviour without needing to wake up and take responsibility for it.

Replace Humiliation with Honour

The experiences of Buff 'n' Puff' and Link 'n' Sink, and others like them, can cause us to sample a difficult emotion. It is not an emotion that we like to admit to, but because of its power, it can cause us endless harm if we do not address it. That emotion is humiliation.

Who likes to admit that they feel humiliated? This emotion brings with it a feeling of failure, of helplessness and the reactionary feelings of anger, bitterness, revenge – which catch us up in the disappointing outcome cycle. You may have felt humiliated at eight years old by a teacher in front of your classmates. You may feel you did something stupid at the age of 15 and got laughed at by people who you were desperately trying to impress. If you are resonating with and recognise the feeling of humiliation, you need to rewrite the root story that you are identifying with. Remember that we do the best we can with the level of knowledge we have at the time. So if you didn't know how to answer that person who laughed at you, or how to act to say 'no' to abuse, or what your legal rights were at the time you were being taken for a ride, forgive yourself for not knowing.

Use the feeling of humiliation to empower yourself instead. See it as the springboard to self-knowledge and that it was showing you there was something you had to learn about valuing yourself. Ask yourself the question, 'How much do I value myself now?' Take some time out to consider and even write down all the ways in which you are valuable to yourself and others. Then take direct action to overwrite your experience of humiliation by doing something simple yet powerful to celebrate the value you bring into the world.

Simple Ways to Celebrate Yourself

➤ Treat yourself to a bath with beautiful and uplifting essential oils such as bergamot, grapefruit or lemon, or deeply sensual flower oils such as neroli, ylang-ylang or rose. Take your time, switch off your devices and make sure you will not be disturbed.

➤ Go and let nature nourish you. Take a walk and breathe in the beauty all around you. Spend time really seeing the plants. Look with focused attention at the intricacy of a flower, the structure of a leaf. Take time to wonder at how many eons it took for nature to develop into what you see today.

➤ Place two jars near your front door. Fill one of the jars with coloured crystals and leave the other one empty. Every time you come home, think about how you brought value into the world today; now, transfer a crystal into the empty jar to mark it. Each week notice how many crystals you have transferred from jar to jar.

If we do not feel honoured, this is because we do not believe in ourselves enough. That we are worthy, deserving, good enough, lovable enough, clever enough. We may not express it in words, but our energy shouts it loud for all the world to hear and people will respond accordingly. You do not need to open your mouth for those around you to know how you see yourself and the world. They will mirror it back to you by their actions.

What we think about, we bring about. Do you feel that you are given the time, respect, space, love and appreciation that you deserve? Do you feel supported, guided, heard? If the answer is 'no', then you need an internal overhaul of your belief structures and your energy signature.

In the course of my work with over 1000 clients in my private practice, throughout many countries, one theme stands out.

People are not honouring themselves within their lives. This fact creates unhappiness, illness, disharmony and an inability to view others as valuable and precious beings. It means we are operating at a lower level of life quality than we should be.

I See You

I recently came across the most beautiful and wise way of bringing preciousness into our relationships. It comes from the Zulu, a very sagacious people. They have gained pearls of wisdom and they have kept their treasure, instead of letting it be eroded and forgotten.

Sawubona is a foundational word for the Zulu. Its literal translation is 'I see you', but the concept goes much deeper than that. By it, the Zulu mean 'we see you' *and* your ancestors: it is a profound acknowledgement of our interlinked existence and connection to the Universe, which recognises the dignity and worth of each individual. The traditional response is '*yabu sawubona*', which means, 'Yes, I see you too.' This is the confirmation of people coming together for a sacred moment in time for a special purpose. That purpose is to witness and explore how we can benefit each other's lives.

Sawubona offers an opportunity to discover what we can do together to set each other free from our limitations and realise the full expression of ourselves. It is the time to ask: 'How do I need to be in order for you to be free?' *Sawubona* is a gift given from the most selfless place: from an open heart and a clear understanding that we are more than our physical selves and we are each on an important journey.

Umuntu ngumuntu nagabantu is the essence of Zulu philosophy and it means 'a person is a person because of other people'. It can be interpreted as: 'I did not exist before you saw me, your recognition brought me into being.' Do you remember the double-slit experiment I described in the Personal Energy Principle 4? The inevitable conclusion of the experiment was that the observer affects the observed, which was discovered in a laboratory by scientists. Yet the Zulu have known this deep wisdom for centuries. It is reflected in the way they honour each other though this profound greeting of *sawubona*.

We could do with a lot more of this honouring in the world, but it takes one important thing to be able to do it. We need to be able to honour each other's presence as valuable and precious beings. A good starting point is through the practice of deep listening.

Deep Listening

Most conversations are not really conversations; they are two people talking at one another without any comprehension of each other. This is where loneliness, dissociation and depression can arise.

One of the least developed skills of many of us is that of deep listening. Yet it is one of the greatest gifts we can give someone. To hold sacred space for them to be able to express themselves without judgement and with respect. People pay fortunes to just be heard by someone professional. However, I practise deep listening with conscious intention every day and it goes hand-in-hand with the art of non-assumption, which you will learn about in Global Energy Principle 23. Try it out.

Deep listening means that you are consciously engaged with whoever you are having a conversation with. It means that you are actively focused on them, on what they say, what they omit and how their energy feels. You are not distracted by what you want to say next, or by your own opinions about a subject. You set that aside and honour the other person by being fully present to them. If you have never done this before, you will be amazed at how people will open up to you and feel joyful, excited, engaged with life, or comforted, held and safe in your presence. I repeat: deep listening is one of the greatest gifts you can give another person and it will benefit your own wellbeing at the same time. Combine it with gratitude for magical results.

Practise Gratitude

Create a new habit. Take the following statement of intention into your life and use it. Say it to yourself and start using it with others:

> 'Thank you for the blessing of your presence and existence.'

You might feel very embarrassed at the beginning, but that is because in general we are unused to engaging with that high level of generosity of spirit. However, when you honour someone with such a gift, it can be the catalyst for their deep inner empowerment.

Relationship Energy Principle 17

Beware of energy tramps.

I magine a human hurricane coming towards you. Whipping up your emotions and shattering your peace of mind. Just because you cannot see what is happening does not mean that it isn't. Imagine having a pair of special energy specs that could show you this disruption and the hit your biofield is taking from someone who is an energy tramp.

An energy tramp is someone who is aware that they do not bring calm or happiness or harmony with them into an environment. Someone who does not do any inner work on themselves but just expects others to deal with their behaviour. Usually they are suffering from unexpressed and unbearable emotional pain and they do not know how to deal with it.

Look at it this way: you know how when you have injured yourself or are suffering from an illness, you feel dragged down by physical pain. Sometimes you can't sleep because of it and it fills your mind so that you can't enjoy anything properly. Yet if I asked you to put your finger on where it hurts, you could show me straight away. But what if that pain is emotional distress? The pain can be just as acute and can disrupt someone's life, but they have nowhere to point to show where it hurts. Often we can end up on the receiving end of their emotional distress instead.

Understand that when a person is hurting, sometimes their only way of expressing that pain is by lashing out at others. Don't take it personally. Notice the pain in their eyes and respond with your heart, not your head.

By reading this book and becoming energy aware, you can identify those whirlwinds when they come towards you – and also the whirlwinds you carry with you that affect others.

Surviving an Energy Tramp

A couple of years ago, I was a member of a choir where I had the opportunity to observe how destructive one person's behaviour can be. Like an unexploded bomb, this individual would arrive every week and start vibrating her disruptive energy. She lived through her wounds. Living through your wounds means that you describe yourself as a survivor or sufferer of a particular problem in any given situation.

This member held the other members of the choir hostage by using her wounds to excuse herself from those things she didn't want to do, and demanding preferential treatment for those activities that she did want to take part in. This meant that others missed out on opportunities that they had the talent for. She also used gossip to colour other people's opinions of particular members, because she felt jealous of them. This created arguments, bad feelings and distrust in the group.

The most extreme form of her behaviour came during a three-day workshop. It was as if we had a toddler with us. She threw tantrums if she didn't get her own way, was over-competitive and made hurtful remarks, upsetting others. This was the mind showing itself at its most unruly and untamed; this woman was a total hostage of her mind, her fear-based thinking and explosive emotions. She would not let anyone advise her and she treated kindness with contempt. She was not ready for relationships with another person or social group. She was an energy tramp.

She brought her own unresolved emotional baggage and distorted thinking into a place where hard-working people went to relax and switch off. They turned up every week to get away from the many trials and tribulations in their own lives. They wanted to have fun and create something great by collaborating as a team. But this member took no responsibility for her own choices, brought along her dirty energy every week and made it everyone else's problem.

When members of the police are trained in armed response, they are taught to reassess the situation after every shot. They must learn to identify the threat and the non-threat. They are trained to make a choice in every moment and to be aware of all of the factors affecting their response. They are taught to use the

151

same senses as an animal that is always aware of its environment and reacts appropriately to all new situations. If we adopt the same vigilance in our own lives, we can prevent becoming an emotional hostage.

Let's return to that troubled woman in the choir. So what happened in the end? Personal circumstances meant that I left the choir, but I heard from a friend about the fallout a few months later. Just before a big concert, in which she was due to perform a solo, the woman threatened to leave. She demanded to be able to wear her own dress at the concert instead of the choir colours. As a result, the choir leader became extremely distressed, because, of course, she was an emotional hostage to the woman. Moreover, the leader was obsessed with what others thought of her and took it as a personal slight whenever anyone left the choir. She gave in and allowed the woman to wear her own dress – even though she was the only one to stand out. Then the disruptive individual left the choir anyway a few weeks after the performance.

If the other members of the choir had been aware of the vibrational dynamics, she would not have been able to behave as a disruptor. Each person would have recognised what she was doing and responded appropriately. But they were there to relax, so were probably not prepared for a highly toxic challenge. That made them vulnerable, especially if they carried unresolved issues of their own.

This is another reason why it is better to deal with your own emotional baggage and logical limiters. To know your own energy signature. You will then know instantly if someone else is aiming to use their energy to control or alter you. Your inner compass will stay pointing north.

Relationship Energy Principle 18

Become aware of the need to engage in any punishment
and protection behaviours and release yourself from these.

When I work with my clients, I sometimes find that there is an underlying reason for why they attract disappointing and unhappy outcomes to themselves. On checking into their biofield, I discover that their mind has set up a punishment or protection response that kicks in when they try to create something good in their life. These two responses can become very debilitating. But why should our minds build these two barriers to our wellbeing? As with practically everything, the answer lies in the past.

Punishment

Punishment behaviour can occur in two ways. The first is self-flagellation, when we are punishing ourselves and may therefore put ourselves on a starvation diet by denying ourselves abundance and wellbeing. Alternatively, we may end up punishing someone else, which is when others can get caught up in our vengeful behaviour and become our collateral damage.

Self-flagellation

When things go wrong in our lives, instead of putting the blame outside ourselves, we may be tempted to turn the blame on ourselves. This is a highly destructive way of disempowering ourselves, as it prevents us from both learning from the experience and finding a healthy solution to the fall-out from it.

Our mind's number 1 need is to be proved right, so we create situations in our outer reality that reflect our beliefs. If we are beating ourselves up about an experience and we fall into a negative mindset about ourselves, we will recreate that negative pattern in our lives. If we feel on some level that we do not deserve to be happy, healthy, successful or loved, we never will be any of these things until we change that mindset.

If we do not forgive ourselves for our shortcomings, we are effectively telling our minds that we deserve to be punished. Once we have created that vibration, punishment will be attracted into our lives. This could be in the form of an abusive partner or a belittling boss. It could be that we always miss out on a great opportunity or that we deny ourselves anything that gives pleasure. Because we are playing out our negative beliefs, we often push away anyone who tries to change them or challenge them.

If you recognise this behaviour in yourself, examine those situations in the past which make you feel uncomfortable about yourself. Look through an honest lens and see the truth of that memory. Get past the warped perspective your mind has created. Examine your actions and observe the context in which things happened. Understand that you did the best you could at the time with the skills and information that you had then. Accept yourself for who you were then – and let it go. You are not that person now and you have a choice to be who you want to be.

Punishing others

This behaviour happens when we can't forgive someone for the harm we perceive they have done to us. We want to make them pay for it. We can be awkward and say no just to make them unhappy and irritated. Maybe when we are asked to do something, we make a deliberate mistake with it. How dare anyone ask us to do anything!

When we are caught in this punishment cycle, we can be cruel, cynical, sullen and even hostile towards others. The trouble is that this behaviour can get out of control. Anger and hatred are like an emotional cancer; they can spread and destroy every part of our lives. Maybe we feel unappreciated or cheated by life and just want to lash out at someone. This is because we have not processed the pain from the past and we do not know how to express it now.

The real sadness is that if you feel like this, you are hurting yourself and shutting yourself off from love. You will not let anyone reach you, because your anger and resentment are the fuel for the fire of righteous indignation. This is one of the worst states in which to make any decisions, because you are likely to sabotage yourself as your mind is on a rampage and intent on adding as much fuel to that fire as it can to justify the anger.

To break the cycle, be totally honest with yourself: how did things really happen in the past? Unravel your emotions and set them in the place they belong. Then work on forgiving others and yourself, and release yourself from this bondage.

Protection

Protective behaviours are another way in which we may be hampering our own happiness and fulfilment. As with punishment, protection can be focused either internally or externally, as I will explain.

Invisibility

When we have been hurt, exploited and treated badly in the past, this can stop us from trying to improve our lives. Maybe it leaves us wanting to blend into the background and not be noticed. This, in turn, can set up contradictions and internal conflict. We desperately want to change. We want to do all of those healthy things that we know we should, but somehow we just don't do them...

One way in which this behaviour can show up is with a wish to lose weight. I have worked with many clients who wanted to get fitter, slimmer and stop eating comfort food. I have found that sometimes the reason they are blocked from losing weight is because their mind sees it as a threat. They may have had an abusive or unhappy relationship in the past. If they lose weight they will become attractive. If they become attractive they will be vulnerable to another relationship, where they will get hurt and abused again. So there is a resistance set up in order to protect against that outcome.

The past hurt and fear need to be dealt with in order to be able to drop the hunger for further protection. Just because you have had bad experiences in the past does not mean things will be the same now. That is why you need to deal with all your emotional baggage and logical limiters before making any decisions.

Being a guard dog

When we have given up on our own dreams and our goals in the past, it is compelling to live out those dreams and goals through someone else, whom we see as having the chance to fulfil them. Because those dreams and goals are dear to us, we can mistakenly think that someone else has the same dreams and goals as us. We can end up acting like a guard dog around the nurturing of those desires.

It's almost like tending a garden that belongs to someone else: we will do anything to see those desires of ours fulfilled and we may restrict the other person from following their own path. We 'protect' them from themselves because we do not want them to make the same mistakes we made. We think that if the other person does not fulfil our dreams and goals as their own, then it is a mistake that they will suffer for.

Sometimes parents fall into this pattern of behaviour, which is unhealthy both for them and their child. We can never know the path someone is here to take in this lifetime. In Relationship Energy Principle 19, I will be talking about our soul heritage. There are underlying patterns in our lives that are individual to each of us. Everyone has their own dreams and goals – and we need to respect these. If you have given up on your own dreams and goals, work to reconnect with them and do everything you can to fulfil them. Nourish your own life and find the joy of achievement.

If you recognise that punishment or protection behaviours are restricting you from making Bright Choices, it is time to dissolve the need for them in your mind. You will find solutions for how to do this in the Energy Aware tools section on pages 207–18 at the back of this book.

156

Relationship Energy Principle 19

By sitting in judgement against another person, you are sitting in judgement against yourself. We have all been everyone at one time or another. We are all reflections of the same energy.

Quantum physics has 'discovered' something that is ancient knowledge, and that is the fact that we are all connected by invisible threads of energy. An ancient maxim states that 'All is One'. Physicists call this phenomenon 'quantum entanglement'. When subatomic particles such as photons interact with each other and are then separated in space, an energetic connection still remains. The distance can be enormous; they can even be in two different galaxies, billions of light years away. Yet no matter the distance between them, that connection endures. Furthermore, what affects one affects the other, instantly. Scientists are still unsure of the nature of that eternal bond. Albert Einstein was so annoyed about the quantum entanglement phenomenon that he called it 'spooky action at a distance'.

There is an eye-opening experiment I would like to tell you about, which has far-reaching implications. Some cheek cells were taken from a Vietnam War veteran and sent to a laboratory several miles away. The volunteer was then connected up to a stress monitor and sat in front of a screen. Images were flashed on the screen which periodically contained upsetting images from the Vietnam War. Several miles away, his cheek cells had also been connected up to a stress monitor It was found that as soon as the volunteer became upset and registered a stress reaction, his cheek cells showed the same reaction.

It is not just our cells that react in this way; the whole energy of any living being in our environment also reacts to how we think and behave. When I say 'the environment', I don't just mean your immediate living space – I mean our Earth and the Universe itself. I know that it is a mind-blowing concept, but quantum entanglement is a real phenomenon. When we add this together with the fact that energy cannot be created or destroyed, you begin to see a very different world emerging through the cracks of what you have been told is true about how life works.

I want to open you up to the possibility that our relationships sometimes do not start when we meet someone. Occasionally, it is as if something already exists between ourselves and another person; an unspoken understanding even if we have only just met them. However, it's possible that we actually haven't just met them at all! Rather, we may have a long history of shared experiences in previous lifetimes. You might be picking up on centuries' worth of soul history that you have experienced with them.

I call this 'soul heritage' and it can be very complicated. It can involve shared love and also hate, which our conscious minds have no understanding of. When someone drives you insane and has a huge impact on you, or you are deeply in love with them, this can indicate the likelihood of a shared soul heritage.

The Eternal Archive

Mystics and sages have long maintained there exists an interconnecting field at the roots of reality that records and carries information. This field is known as the Akashic records. The word 'Akasha' comes from a Sanskrit word meaning 'ether', 'air' or the medium of movement.

Recent discoveries in quantum physics now show that this Akashic field exists and is a sea of photons of light known as the energy matrix. What we think of as static space is actually filled with tiny particles of energy, which are known as subatomic particles. This subtle sea of fluctuating energies is where all matter arises from. Our consciousness also arises from the energy matrix.

The energy matrix is not only the source of all original matter that manifests in time and space, but is also the constant and enduring memory of the Universe and everything in it. It holds the vibrational record of everything that has happened and everything that has the potential of happening. This includes the information about all of your past incarnations and soul heritage. I call these soul-print memories. Your biofield is the database of your existence, the information field of your soul.

Our Soul Families

Reading the eternal energetic data from the biofields of over 1000 clients has enabled me to build up a picture of who we are from the vibrations that permeate our Universe. Just as we belong to an earthly family, we also belong to a soul group family. The members of your soul group family are likely to have incarnated with you lifetime after lifetime. When you are between lives, your incorporeal essence makes choices, including with whom you will incarnate the next lifetime. As I have come to understand it, you and the members of your soul group family all have a signature vibration, which is one note in the harmonic spectrum that identifies your soul tribe.

The size of a soul group family is indeterminate; as far as I am aware, scientific capabilities have not yet been turned to exploring the subject. My work with my clients has revealed that the members of our family, romantic partners and best friends are often also members of our soul group family. Sometimes we have made an agreement to experience a lifetime with someone who belongs to another soul group family, and often this is for a specific reason.

Not long after I started exploring soul heritage issues with clients, I came across two authors who had written books that underpinned what I had discovered through my work in the biofield. Michael Newman and Brian Weiss both work with past-life regression techniques. They access the time between lives with their patients, where choices are made for our next incarnations. In their books, they describe the memories that their patients began to recall from the time before they were incarnated in this life. These include recognitions of soul family members echoing back through eons of time. I found many confirmations that matched up with the data I was discovering using my Life Retuning techniques.

Lessons in Love

We choose to incarnate with particular members of our soul group in order to experience the challenges and triumphs of love – either the presence or the absence of it. We choose to experience love in all its forms: romantic, familial, friendships, with our pets and wild animals and unconditional love. We may incarnate over several lifetimes with the same soul family members, but have different relationships with them. The same soul can incarnate as our mother, father, brother, sister or our partner during the course of our lifetimes.

We can recognise the energy of a soul mate by looking into their eyes – there is often a jolt of electricity experienced by both people. The telepathic connection is very strong here on Earth and if our energy is clear enough of our own emotional baggage, it is possible to pick up on a soul mate's thoughts, emotions and physical states.

Remember what happened to the cheek cells of the volunteer. We can be quantumly entangled over many lifetimes. Your biofield is the repository for specific information about your soul family members and who you were to each other in your past lives.

Intriguing evidence comes from the work of Dr Ian Stevenson. For 37 years, he travelled the world, documenting over 2000 cases of children who remembered their past lives. Some of them wanted to go back to the family they had been part of before they died. Some of them recalled the place they had lived and went back there and correctly identified people they had known. There were those who had a birthmark exactly where their previous incarnation had a fatal injury to their physical body.

These cases cannot be ignored. This is a vast arena of discussion, which we lack the space to delve into in these pages, but the important thing to know is that we have had many lives and therefore have all experienced poverty, luxury, failure and success. So when you make a judgement about someone else and their way of life, remember that you have been there too. If it wasn't in this lifetime, you can bet you experienced it in a past life.

Part Three: **Planetary Currents**

We have been looking at our human world, the interactions we have with each other and the intricate, multilevel complexities of our behaviour and reactions and the primal undercurrents that drive us. You now know that you are a vibrational being. From your cells to your thoughts, from your emotions to your biofield, you use electricity, light, sound and heat every moment of your life.

So it is time to pull back the focus to gain a view of our magnificent and extraordinary planet – and to draw your attention to the background energetic landscape that shapes everything on Earth, including us. You already know about some of the other species that share our planet with us and which have evolved capabilities to harness natural energies, and that they use these abilities without question to thrive. Let me now open your eyes and your ears to just how much of a vibrational world you live in.

Our Magnificent Earth

Sacred texts called the Vedas were written in Sanskrit around 1500 BC by an ancient civilization that lived in the Indus Valley region of South Asia. These texts talk about the primordial sound that all of creation originates from a primal acoustic vibration that brought about our Universe and everything in it. The scriptures identify this sound as 'Aum'.

Recent missions into space have reported that each of the planets has a unique song, a frequency of emissions, which you can listen to on NASA YouTube videos. So what about Earth? Our planet is surrounded by a Van Allen belt – a circle of electromagnetically charged particles, some of which come from the solar wind, emanating from the sun. These particles have an electrical charge exceeding 30,000,000 volts. It is estimated that the Earth's Van Allen belt stretches at least 20,000 km into space. There are radio wave recordings by NASA of what it sounds like. They are referred to as chorus waves and sound like rising and swooping whistling.

Have you ever come across a retro sixties children's programme called *The Clangers*? When I first saw it, I remember thinking how weird yet enigmatic the sounds were that they were using for the characters' communication. Imagine my surprise when I first heard a recording of the sounds made by Earth, because they brought the programme to mind. Did the programme makers know something back then that even NASA didn't?

If we take our attention from the space surrounding our Earth and dive down through the atmosphere, we find that acoustic waves come in different guises. I want to give you an overview of how the sound spectrum affects you. Did you know that you can never experience complete silence? Even if you were in a room insulated from all sound from outside, your bodily functions, including your breathing, would still create acoustic vibrations. Sound is constantly affecting you, even when it is outside of the range of what you can hear.

And the Walls of Jericho Came Tumbling Down

In the chapter 'The Wise Child Inside You', I described how the torpedo ray kills its prey by shocking it to death with electricity. Another creature of the seas kills with sound. The tiny pistol shrimp has an oversized claw which it snaps when it is ready for lunch. Its snapping claw creates a cavitation bubble, which sends out a deadly shockwave that travels at more than 100 kph at a sound level of 218 decibels. For just one millisecond this heats the water to the same temperature as the surface of the sun! Lunch doesn't stand a chance.

You may know the Old Testament story of how Joshua had his men play their trumpets outside the walls of the city of Jericho and the sound made the walls collapse so that they could invade the place. Sound can be used as a very effective weapon. For years, scientists were puzzled by the unusual effect a roaring lion has on its prey. When the lion gives a deep, guttural roar, instead of instantly fleeing, animals are momentarily paralyzed, giving the lion a brief opportunity to strike. Even lion trainers can go into shock when lions utter this sound. The big cat is using infrasound. This is a low-frequency blast that the prey actually feels as well as hears. We can hear soundwaves between 20 to 20,000 Hz, but this part of the lion's roar falls below our range of hearing at 18 Hz. The roar is the attack before the kill. It is so powerful that it can cause disorientation and momentarily stun an animal.

Other animals also use infrasound to communicate, including elephants, whales, hippopotami, rhinos, giraffes and the okapi. But it is not just creatures that create low frequency vibrations. Volcanoes emit infrasound before they erupt, which is used by volcanologists to predict when they will go critical. In 2015, a volcano called Cotopaxi near Quito in Ecuador started to emit a very strange sound. The actual sound is too low for us to hear, but has been translated into an audible register and sounds like someone is breathing in and out while sleeping deeply. The real slumbering fire mountain!

Infrasound can travel long distances, permeating buildings, cutting through dense forests, and even passing through mountains. The lower the frequency, the farther the distance the sound can travel.

Let's now go to the other end of the sonic scale – to the sound frequencies that are too high for us to hear.

The Sonic Bounce Back

Bats hunt using a method called echolocation. They emit ultrasonic acoustic waves in frequencies of about 12 kHz to 160 kHz through their nose or mouth, which creates a landscape of sound. The ultrasonic waves echo back the information to the bat about its environment. The sound pressure of these waves ranges between 60 to 140 decibels.

The bat can hear its prey but sometimes it enters into a battle that seems more like something out of *Star Wars*! A bat's favourite food is the moth; however, some moths such as the garden tiger moth emit their own ultrasound and jam the bat's frequency. Have you ever wondered why some moths have such thick fur? It is used to confuse and distort the soundwaves of a hunting bat.

Ultrasound is so powerful that we have developed many ways of using it. It is utilised in medicine to break up kidney stones, to perform pregnancy scans and for cancer detection. There is one use that may revolutionise how we clean our teeth. In 1992, a gadget was invented by Robert T. Bock, which brought ultrasound even further into our everyday lives. Ultrasonic toothbrushes emit ultrasonic waves at high frequency vibrations. The waves dislodge plaque without the need for any brushing. For a toothbrush to be regarded as ultrasonic, it has to emit waves at a minimum of 20,000 Hz or 2,400,000 vibrations or movements every minute. In the United States, an ultrasonic toothbrush should have a minimum frequency of 1.6 Megahertz, which is equivalent to 192,000,000 oscillations per minute. I wonder how moths and bats will be affected if it becomes popular to have one. Perhaps the hunter won't be able to find the prey anymore, as instead of the moth, we will be jamming their frequency instead.

Soundwaves cause vibrations in the air and therefore create movement. However there is a completely different type of energy wave, which includes the visible colours you can see. As I have mentioned, colours are specific frequencies of light and light comes into the category of electromagnetic energy. This type of energy can shift between being a subatomic particle such as an electron and a wave of energy with no mass. The electromagnetic spectrum starts at one end with radio waves, which are the longest waves and use the least amount of energy, through to microwaves, infrared radiation, the visible light spectrum, ultraviolet radiation, X-rays and gamma radiation, which has the fastest and shortest waves.

The diagram below shows the distribution of the full electromagnetic spectrum that we are aware of to date.

Radio waves Microwaves Infrared   Visible Light Ultraviolet X-rays Gamma rays
The electromagnetic spectrum

As you can see, the visible light spectrum makes up a tiny part of the full spectrum; the rest is invisible to the naked eye. Because it is hidden, it is easy to forget or not believe that it exists. However, tremendous power resides in the unseen parts of the electromagnetic spectrum. It is so important that you understand what these invisible energies are, because technology is using them and you are bathed in them from unnatural sources, but more about that later.

X-rated and 'G' Force

The short waves of X-rays are found in nature in lightning, exploding supernovae and in the plasma discharge from our sun. They sit at the high frequency end of the electromagnetic spectrum. They emit ionising radiation, which means that they create free radicals that can be damaging for our bodies if we have too much exposure to them. They are used in a medical capacity to see inside the body and by scientists to discover the elemental makeup of substances.

Gamma rays have the shortest wavelength known at this time and are found across the Universe. They are produced by the most violent explosions from neutron stars, mass ejections from our sun, pulsars and black holes. On Earth, natural gamma rays are found in lightning bolts. Their wavelength is so short that they can pass through atoms without being detected. They can kill living cells but thankfully – apart from the threat of man-made nuclear explosions or a direct lightning strike – we are not usually in danger from them.

The Living Spark

At the start of this book, I mentioned something that many of us have done. As a child you probably rubbed a balloon on your T-shirt and then had fun seeing your hair sticking to it. Or perhaps you put the balloon on the wall and you were amazed that it just stayed there. Have you ever touched something metal and received an electric shock? In both cases you were experiencing

165

static electricity, the build-up of an invisible force. When that force connects with something else that is a conductor, like your body, it creates a spark.

Lightning happens because of the same principle. A storm cloud builds up an electrostatic charge and then that electricity has to discharge. This happens when the electricity finds a route to connect with other charged clouds or down to connect with the Earth and then travels back up.

A typical lightning flash is about 300 million volts and about 30,000 amps. Occasionally, when it strikes the ground, it can fuse the soil and if this contains sand, the strike vitrifies this into glass tubes that stretch down into the earth. These tubes are called fulgurites and some of them have a curious resemblance to pieces of bleached coral. The pattern of a lightning bolt with its snaking branches that rip the sky with searing light are echoed in the fused stone. Many fulgurites have smaller and smaller branches. What we are seeing is the fractal pattern inherent in much of nature. A bolt of lightning can emit X-rays and gamma rays, along with the visible flash of light, and the temperature of the air around it can reach between 20,000 to 30,000°F, which is hotter than the surface of the sun.

The Ultraviolet Club

I have known for a long time that there is something very special about ultraviolet light. At the start of Part One, I described the experiments that Fritz Alfred Popp conducted into how various substances scrambled ultraviolet light or reflected it back at the same frequency of light. I also mentioned that it is well known that you can blast a living cell with a beam of high intensity ultraviolet light and destroy it. If, afterwards, you direct a weak beam of the same light at the same cell, it will repair 99 per cent of itself in just one day.

Clearly, we have a very special relationship with this form of light energy. As with the other invisible waves of electro-magnetic radiation, ultraviolet light is found across the Universe, most especially when young stars are being formed. On Earth, many insects can see ultraviolet light and some creatures use it to distinguish between individuals. In 2018, it was discovered that the bones of chameleons glow blue through their skin under ultraviolet light. Equally, many creatures in the sea use ultraviolet light – the shells of sea turtles glow and deep sea fish such as the angler fish use it for hunting.

A cutting-edge experiment carried out in 2020 by the Department of Environmental Sciences and Natural Resources in Wisconsin came to the astonishing conclusion that the bill of the platypus glows green and blue. Just two months later, Toledo Zoo revealed that their Tasmanian devils also glow blue. They have gone on to discover that many of the marsupials and mammals in Australia also have glowing blue fur. Bioluminescence is the ability to absorb UV light and then re-emit it as blue light, which is what we can see happening with these animals. We now know that fish, birds, reptiles, amphibians and even mammals use bioluminescence, which shows up under ultraviolet light. We could be forgiven to start feeling a little left out of the ultraviolet club!

Just Because We Can, Doesn't Mean We Should…

John Dee was the court astronomer for, and advisor to, Queen Elizabeth I in the sixteenth century. He was very knowledgeable about mathematics, astronomy and the burgeoning science of alchemy, which became chemistry. He believed that every entity in the Universe emanated 'rays' of force which influenced the other objects they struck. I wonder what he would have thought about the electromagnetic emissions that our technological devices use. He would probably be running away very fast from us! I am sure he would have seen the inherent folly in bathing our biological bodies in electromagnetic waves that are outside of our natural frequencies.

In the late 1990s, WiFi was invented. People started carrying devices that were not only physically interactive when our fingers pressed buttons to send instant messages, but which became interactive on a deeper level as well. This level was unseen and unknown about for a long time by the general public. Gradually, technology companies were increasingly harnessing the electromagnetic energy waves of the invisible spectrum.

Mobile phones work by receiving and emitting microwave and radio wave frequencies. Our world has become more and more saturated with artificial energy – until now it is hardly possible to take a breath without being constantly irradiated with frequencies that are beyond those that humans have experienced over thousands of years.

In 2016, I read a book that opened my eyes to the inadequacies of commercial research being done into the safety of the mobile phones that many people carry in their pockets, bras and bags. The dubious power of the laptops that sit looking so innocuous on our tables and in our laps was discussed in a way that stopped me in my tracks. The book that sparked my interest was called *The Non-Tinfoil Guide to EMFs* by investigative health journalist Nicolas Pineault. The author did a lot of research into a topic that was not popular at the time, because it was an inconvenient truth. Let's face it, who wants to curtail the leisure of tapping an icon, swiping or scrolling and getting instant access to mental fast food? Fast food is addictive and so is fast mental gratification. Mobile phones have become like a phantom limb and many people can't bear being without them.

We live in a world where more and more satellites are beaming unnatural energy at us, and our homes are being upgraded into alien AI hives. We should be disturbed about what is happening to our physical bodies and our minds. Do you remember the Borg in *Star Trek*? Like them, we too are being assimilated.

Today, you can cheerfully take a radiation kit with you everywhere you go. You get to sit in dirty energy and dangerous hot spots – and you don't even know it. At night, if you keep your router on, you sleep in the low frequency buzz of emanations that have never been adequately tested for human health. Do you keep your mobile switched on, on the bedside table next to your head, just in case you get a phone call during the night? Those unseen electromagnetic waves are affecting the natural electricity in the cells in your body, your brainwaves and your biofield.

In 2011, the International Agency for Research on Cancer, part of the World Health Organisation, issued a press release classifying cell phone radiation as a Type-2B carcinogen. That means that your phone is not your friend. Despite this warning, research showed that in 2019 the highest sales of fridge freezers were made at 2 am! Surfing and buying online prevents many people from getting healthy sleep.

This book is called *Energy Aware* because I want to give you as much information as I can about the energetic world you live in and that you are interconnected with. It is therefore important for you to know that technology has an impact on your physical health, mental health and even your moods. In his book *EMF Practical Guide*, Lloyd Burrell rounds up what electromagnetic frequencies, or EMFs, do to us when we use them every day. He catalogues the ever-increasing body of scientific evidence, which is revealing a less than happy scene for us as humans as we continue to use more and more of this powerful energy.

Hot Stuff

On the other end of the electromagnetic spectrum, beyond visible light, we find the infrared band. Warm-blooded mammals give off heat and the reason for this is found in this part of the electromagnetic spectrum. This is where you find the energy waves that are responsible for why we feel the warmth from the sun. The glare of light from snow is partly made up of infrared waves, which is why we can get sunburnt even when the weather is cold. There is a delicate natural balance between the infrared radiation emitted by our sun and what our Earth absorbs and radiates back out into space. It is called the Earth Radiation Budget. Nature has it sorted!

One range out from infrared is the vibrational domain of microwaves. You probably know about microwaves from the ovens that sit on the kitchen counter and which can heat up food within a couple of minutes. Microwave radiation is able to heat up molecules of water quickly and therefore cooks food much quicker than natural methods. The microwaves force the water and fat in the food to rotate and thereby create heat, which accelerates the normal cooking process.

The effects of microwave radiation emitted from an oven when it is cooking have been measured to extend from 30 to 40 feet. They are also used to carry thousands of phone channels that speed up our ability to make calls on our mobiles and enable us to use GPS in our cars. There is mounting evidence that microwaves at close proximity are able to scramble the electrical impulses in your brain and affect short-term memory. However, in nature, these waves can be found everywhere in space and provide a background radiation that would light up the sky if we were able to see microwaves.

Smart meters and smart devices emit electromagnetic frequencies continuously. The range of these falls in the radio and microwave part of the energy spectrum. Their radiation levels are stronger than a microwave.

You now know about the mounting body of evidence about our use of these energies. How do you think the cells in your body deal with the constant bombardment of much more powerful electromagnetic waves? I believe that as time goes by and more is known about the biofield, we will be in for a shock as to what is really going on with non-biological frequencies.

Let me take you back up from the surface of our planet, out into space, and show you our Earth from a distance. Put on your energy specs and have a look at what you can see. There is a magnetic shield that makes our planet habitable. It deflects the solar wind, which would otherwise eat away at our atmosphere. It exists thanks to the swirling liquid iron and nickel in our planet's outer core, found 1800 miles down from the surface. The magnetic field has its anchor points at the North and South poles. Just like any magnet, the magnetic circuit extends out from them in field lines that surround the Earth in a positive feedback loop.

Magnetic energy is an attractant and repellent force. Magnets have long been known to be able to help our health. The first medical text we know of is the Yellow Emperor's Book of Internal Medicine, written in China around 2000 BC, where the application of magnetic stones is mentioned. The magnetic force is vital for life. In 2018, research done at the Lund University in Sweden revealed that European robins produce a special protein in their eyes called a cryptochrome, which is sensitive to the blue light frequency. It is now thought that this protein enables the birds to see the magnetic lines of the Earth, so those birds that do migrate are able to navigate long distances.

Earth's Electrical Heartbeat

While you are floating there in space looking at the Earth, just take a quiet moment. Do you feel a regular pulse emanating from our planet? You have probably heard of the Schumann resonance. It is known as the Earth's heartbeat and it is an electrical frequency; a regular resonance that is constantly being produced. The general consensus is that it has been at 7.83 Hz for a long time and that now it is shifting to over 8 Hz. However, the biometeorologists who measure these things will tell you that there are actually a range of measurements and the 7.83 Hz has been the strongest.

Let's revisit lightning now, because it has one more special surprise in store for you! The first important thing to note is that the Schumann resonance is made up of the background electrical zaps that come from lightning bolts around the globe. It has been found that every second, there are at least 100 that strike the ground. The electrical strikes of lightning bolts emit ELFs, which are Extremely Low Frequencies found in the radio wave part of the electromagnetic spectrum. These waves have a range of 3 to 30 Hz, much lower than the frequencies your mobile phone uses.

A recent study published by the *Journal of Biometeorology* puts forward the idea that these frequencies match with the background electrical activity in living cells. The standard electricity of the cells of both vertebrates and invertebrates is between 5 and 45 Hz. About 20 years ago, the discovery was made that many biological systems, including our brains, have electrical activity in exactly the same frequency range as that produced by global lightning activity. Scientists are now flirting with the idea that it is possible that life on Earth evolved to harness these natural background frequencies. Having worked with the biofield for many years, in my opinion it is much more than possible; I'd say it was obvious. Biological systems always use the most available resources in order to evolve and thrive. Harnessing the most abundant electrical energy on our planet would make total sense. Perhaps Frankenstein's monster was not such a far-fetched idea after all! The fact is that we live electrically and we also affect the Earth with our electrical emanations. Electricity is our birthright.

The Hertz in Our Hearts

Take your attention back to yourself, to the beating centre of your life. I have already revealed that your heart is so much more than just an organ that pumps the blood around your body. You now know that it has an electrical field that has been measured to be 5000 times more powerful than that of your brain.

Some incredible research has been done over the last few years by leading scientists at the HeartMath Institute into the correlation between our Earth's magnetic fields and how they affect our health, behaviour and consciousness. From a different viewpoint than NASA and the weather researchers, the HeartMath team have found that there is a symbiotic relationship between living beings and our planet. This reaches peak efficiency when heart coherence is achieved. Heart coherence is when our thoughts and emotions are brought into sync with our heart energy. What I have described as the empowered choice cycle and Bright Choices in Part One of this book will enable us to achieve that state of coherence.

Each of us is contributing our own unique vibration to the interconnected field of energies of our planet. The electromagnetic field of our hearts is the driving force that brings our vibrations into a harmonious state. Because we affect each other and the Earth, it is very important that the vibrations we are contributing are positive and aligned with life-enhancement. When the raw energy of lightning strikes, it magnetically attracts the electricity from the Earth from high points and from living beings, including humans. We are all attractants for energy.

Working in conjunction with the Global Coherence Initiative, the findings of the HeartMath Institute reveal how when we have a coherent, positive emotional and mental state en masse, we can create a great magnetic force for peace, wellbeing and a healthy environment. There is now a vast global experiment taking place involving thousands of people around our planet. Magnetic field monitors have been positioned in several countries that measure the global fluctuations of Earth's magnetic field. The Global Coherence Initiative is researching how our collective consciousness affects it. It aims to create nothing less than a massive shift in global consciousness.

Making Bright Choices gets us to this state of optimum heart and energetic coherence. It is clear that up-levelling the quality of the decisions and choices we all make now will shape our planetary future. In this part of the book, I am going to share with you the Global Energy Principles. They will guide you to live in an energetically informed and globally aware way.

Global Energy Principle 20

Become a Guardian of Consciousness.

I believe that fairy tales are not for children – they are to remind adults of universal truths. Children don't need reminding; they instinctively know as their deep inner knowing has not been hijacked as yet. Fairy tales hold powerful metaphors and archetypal aspects. Cultural memories are encapsulated within stories that trigger us at a deep unconscious level. One fairy tale has echoes of the current global situation as we step into the New Era. It is the tale of Sleeping Beauty. First, though, for a little bit of context...

Our Earth has a wobble, caused by the tilt of the planet's axis, which results in an observable phenomenon called the precession of the equinoxes. Because of this wobble, the constellations in the sky appear to rotate around the Earth, each taking a turn to rise behind the sun on the vernal equinox. It takes almost 26,000 years to complete a cycle.

The Hindus believe that this cycle can be broken up into ages called Yugas, each with a particular characteristic. During half of the cycle, humans are falling asleep in consciousness and forgetting the truth; and for the other half of the cycle, we are waking up. Each of the parts of the cycle are tied into specific global events. Right now, we are moving into the part of the cycle where we are starting to wake up, according to the calculations. Sri Yukteswar, a renowned Kriya yogi who died in 1936, calculated that we have now moved from Kali Yuga Devanāgarī, कलियुग (darkness and ignorance), into Dvapara, द्वापर युग (starting to wake up). This also aligns with moving into the Age of Aquarius through precession. We are certainly seeing this change playing out in so many ways.

So Sleeping Beauty is very apt as the fairy story for now. She pricks her finger on the spindle of a spinning wheel (symbolised as the Wheel of Fortune in the Tarot, and also signifying the precession of the ages). The whole castle falls asleep under a spell cast by an evil witch for 100 years, and is covered in thick, impenetrable briars until the Prince arrives to wake Sleeping Beauty up with a kiss. As soon as she wakes up, so does everyone else. Not to be confused with the goddess Kali, Kali Yuga is a demon whose spell we have been under. It is time to regain our personal sovereignty. I see the Prince's kiss as a symbol for the cosmic catalyst. We are being awoken by the kiss of awareness and the activation of our bioenergetic birthright. Then the briars of the Age of Darkness will fall away, leaving us to create our world from a position of heightened consciousness of Dvapara.

Personal sovereignty means reclaiming your spirit from all the places you have given power away to. It is time for you to find all those parts of yourself you gave away, or allowed to be taken, and call them back. Wake up from the spell. Let the briars of darkness and ignorance fall away. Remember who you are as a perfect, magnificent, eternal being of energy and, specifically, of light.

Wake Up to Your True Self

'Though free to think and act, we are held together, like Stars in the firmament, with ties inseparable. These ties cannot be seen, but we feel them. We are all One.'
  – Nikola Tesla, Serbian-American inventor and futurist

My aim throughout this book has been to help you understand how the energy of the planet, and the Universe itself, is the same energy that you have within your physical body. The emanations radiating from your biofield are echoed back to you from your environment. Your thoughts, emotions and actions are part of the eternal fabric of light. It is time to develop the level of respect for this ancient energetic relationship that has existed since the beginning. It is time to make consciousness stand for our vibrational existence. Dust into stars, we are One.

Are you ready to completely transform your life? Are you

ready to let go of the repeating patterns of disappointment you have been living in? Are you fed up of the same old, churned out and regurgitated populist affirmations that get you nowhere? I believe that you are and I am so excited for you and your future. I know what it feels like to wake up and realise that you don't have to do any of that anymore.

It is time to become a very different kind of person, to cross the bridge from the old third-dimension paradigm of life over to the energetic landscape of possibility at a highly evolved level. You now have the pathway set before you.

There are two parts to your journey over the bridge of light. There is the inner work and the outer work. When you are doing both, you become a Guardian of Consciousness and you are actively helping humanity's evolution into Dvapara and the New Era.

The Inner Activist

What do I mean by your 'inner activist'? It means that you proactively deal with those internal issues in your life that you want to change. You take care of your emotional state, your personality, your behaviour and your thought patterns regularly. You do not rely on anyone else to do that work for you. You take full responsibility for your emotions, thoughts, choices and actions.

As a true inner activist, you spend a little bit of time every day checking in with yourself and finding those places that are showing up as needing to be worked on. You are aware of any disharmony. Do you feel a bit angry this morning? Do you feel a little bit demotivated? Are you getting caught up in some self-limiting thoughts about whether you are good enough? You become aware of when you are in danger of being pulled into someone else's drama and you actively create harmony. You do not wait for someone else to rescue you, but equally you immediately recognise when you need to reach out for help and you act on it. You no longer rely on other people's opinions and then get disillusioned by them.

As a true inner activist, you use your biofield to give you the truth of all situations. You practise deep listening and the art of non-assumption, to which I will be introducing you soon, in order to guide yourself through life. As mentioned earlier, at the back of this book, I have created a quick reference table that you can use to check in with yourself and get clear about your emotional and mental state – although it goes much further than that. You will get to be able to read what is happening with your energy and specifically your vortices of light. I have provided you with a series of Energy Aware tools that you can use to get yourself back into harmony.

I am a true inner activist and I have created the quick reference table based on what I do for myself. I start my day by checking through my biofield and dealing with any disharmony before I get up. I check in on where I am at, every morning. I am fully aware of my physical self and my energetic self. I am also fully aware of my positioning in my environment and the status of my inter-actions with the people who were around me yesterday and who will be around me today. I use a couple of Energy Aware tools to set up my vibrational intention for how I want my day to be. None of this takes very long, and you can easily get into a routine just like me. I can tell you it will make all the difference to the quality of your life.

Be an Outer Change Maker

The second part to becoming a Guardian of Consciousness is the outer work – being an outer change maker. This work is to identify where you can be of service in the world, and how you can change your environment for the better. Maybe it is simply to tell somebody else an inspirational story that will give them a boost and help them to do their own inner work, so that they can become empowered in their own life. Maybe it is to allow yourself to be in a place where you have the opportunity to act on your deep inner knowing to be the catalyst for beneficial change.

You will know what it is that you need to do when you pay attention to the primal forces of ebb and flow. For example, you may be at a social event and feel that you are not there to have mundane conversations. Instead, you are there to have a meaningful conversation with a particular person who has uncon-sciously turned up precisely for that reason.

I have done jobs in the past where I've been very aware that I'm not there to do the 'job'; I am there to do the 'other job' or the real work. I once worked at an insurance company as a temp. My 'job' was to retrieve files from the desks of the administrators and put them back in the filing cabinet. Now, you might think that's a deeply boring job. Well, yes, on the surface it was. I had a tiny space that I could call my own. It was a minute cubbyhole that housed all the filing cabinets. There was a table that I would come and put down the stack of case study files on. I could just about walk between the two sides of it.

I had only been there for a couple of days, when people in the office started to visit me in my tiny cubbyhole. It wasn't because they wanted a file. In fact, it wasn't anything to do with the job at all. They came to consult me about issues in their lives that they were worried about. Some of them wanted to know what they could do about their back pain, or how to let go of the fact that they were angry at their partner that morning. Others asked me about what would be the best tea for them to be healthy and what foods were the best for boosting their immunity. Day after day, my 'job' was just a vehicle for me to be able to help those people have a better quality of life. I recognised the signs of why I had been given the opportunity to work there.

When you are an outer change maker, you will recognise the signs too. It is about staying in the stillness of the moment and not allowing your mind to distract you. When I took that temp job, I had no thoughts about being used or exploited, or that surely I could find another job that paid more. None of that matters when you're there for a reason. In this part of the book, you will discover how to use your energy in the wider world too.

Global Energy Principle 21

Live and vibrate on the love frequency.

have mentioned before that words hold power. That whether you are listening to your inner critic or expressing yourself verbally, your thoughts take shape. Your thoughts are electromagnetic and your voice creates an acoustic change in your body and your environment. Sound energy is made by the vibration of air. I have talked about ultrasound and infrasound, and how powerful they are. Even those sound vibrations that you can hear create forms in the physical world. They create incredible shapes that it is possible for us to see.

Cymatics

If you were to take a plate of metal and fix it to a freestanding base, you could see something amazing happen. Imagine pouring a thin layer of sand on the metal plate and then playing a scale of notes in proximity to it. If you watched the sand, it would look like it had suddenly come alive. It would wriggle and twist into beautiful mandalas. Each time you changed the note you were playing, the sand would respond by forming a new pattern. Sometimes, it would form into a central star with symmetrical arcs of sand around it; sometimes, a diamond with four circles around it.

The higher the notes, the more complex and intricate the shapes would become, jumping from parallel lines to a multitude of tiny circles as the wave frequencies became tighter and tighter. As you looked at the patterns, they might remind you of the beautiful paintings that the Aborigines create. They paint the energy in the land and the animals – and you would be struck by the similarities. The shapes of sound surround us all the time.

Using a metal plate and sand is one way to turn sound into matter. This device is known as a Chladni plate and it is used in Cymatics (from the Greek *kyma* or μ , meaning 'wave'), which is the study of visible sound vibration. Typically the surface of a plate, diaphragm or membrane is vibrated, and regions of maximum and minimum displacement are made visible in a thin coating of particles, paste or liquid. In the diagram below, notice how similar the patterns made in water are to a mandala pattern. The underlying shapes of sound have been known about for many centuries.

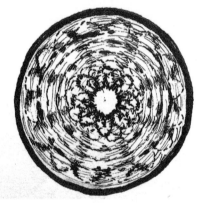

The pattern that the resonance of 528 Hertz makes in water

The pattern of a mandala

The Solfeggio Frequencies and Cymatics

'Concerning matter, we have been all wrong. What we
have called matter is energy, whose vibration has been
so lowered as to be perceptible to the senses. There is no
matter.'
— Albert Einstein, theoretical physicist

In the tenth century, Gregorian monks developed singing a form
of music that came to be known as the Gregorian chant. One
of the most well-known and earliest chants is an eighth-century
poem entitled 'Ut Queant Laxis', a hymn to St John the Baptist.
In it, we find the earliest form of the scales that we know so well
today: Do, Re, Mi, Fa, So, La, Ti, Do. Back then, the notes were
known as Ut, Re, Mi, Fa, Sol, La and the monks sang them as
very particular tones. The chants and their special tones were
believed to impart spiritual blessings when sung in harmony. In
'Ut Queant Laxis', the first six lines of the music were sung one
note higher each time the monks began a new line of the verse:

Ut queant laxis
Resonare fibris,
Mira gestorum
Famuli tuorum,
Solve polluti
Labii reatum,
Sancte Iohannes.

The words can be translated as: 'So that your servants may,
with loosened voices, resound the wonders of your deeds, clean
the guilt from our stained lips, O Saint John.'

The six tones used are known as the Solfeggio frequencies.
They are special tones that have powerful vibrations, which have
been measured as acoustic energy waves. They all resonate with
very particular functions, which are:

➤ 396 Hz – Liberating guilt and fear

➤ 417 Hz – Undoing situations and facilitating change

➤ *528 Hz – Transformation and miracles (DNA repair)*

➤ 639 Hz – Connecting/relationships

➤ 741 Hz – Expression/solutions

➤ 852 Hz – Returning to spiritual order

I have highlighted 528 Hz because this is known as the love frequency. Love is miraculous and transformative. By listening to this tone especially, you can help your mind, body and soul to let go of the disharmonious vibrations that may be keeping you in the disappointing outcome cycle. Love is a life force and it brings you into coherence – as you know from Personal Energy Principle 8. The diagram on page 180 shows the intricate pattern that a sound wave creates in water.

The Solfeggio frequencies were forgotten over time as musicians created new scales. Since the 16th century, we have used the 'twelve-tone equal temperament' tuning system. However, our modern-day musical scale is out of sync when compared with the original Solfeggio scale. It does not give us access to the ancient resonances of activation. I have created a video on my website with 528 Hz which you can access by using the link on page 8.

Just like the Gregorian monks on the other side of the world, the Tibetan monks knew the power of sound. In their temples, they used a very special instrument called a singing bowl. Their bowls were made of metal and when they struck the bowl with a wooden mallet, it would produce a beautiful resonant sound; by running the mallet around the rim, the bowl would start to 'sing'. Each bowl was a particular size and made of a particular mix of metals to produce the exact tone they wanted. Bowls were played to heal different parts of the body and to open up the energy centres in the biofield.

Cymatics shows us that there is no randomness in our world. Those hidden energy waves create patterns and shapes which mould our physical reality. When you make a decision, you set a process into motion. If you follow the energy, the outcome is predictable. That is why it is so important to get your vibration aligned with the best outcome. When you amplify your heart energy and vibrate at that frequency, you activate your heart field and come into a state of coherence. As you know, coherence is the maximum harmonised state where everything in your biofield is vibrating in unity.

Global Energy Principle 22

Notice when synchronicity shows up in your life. It is
showing you that you are in alignment with your highest
path and purpose.

You may have heard the term 'synchronicity' many times
by now. It is one of the words that is having more and
more significance in people's lives. You may be using it
more yourself. At one time, I would not have understood why
seemingly random events would have indicated anything more
than simple coincidence. That was before my life imploded and
I had to rewrite everything from scratch. Then I came across an
ancient maxim: 'as above, so below'.

The maxim made me think of the ancient Egyptians and the
great pyramids of the Giza Plain – especially the three curiously
positioned pyramids of Cheops, Khufu and Khafre. There is a
slight apparent misalignment between the two smaller structures
and now archaeologists propose that they were meant to mirror
the celestial alignment of the stars in the constellation of Orion,
specifically the three stars in what is known as Orion's belt.

The maxim 'as above, so below' is almost as ancient as the
pyramids, having been discovered on an artefact called the
Emerald Tablet, which is supposed to contain the secrets of the
Universe as written by Hermes Trismegistus. This was the name
the ancient Greeks used for Thoth, the Egyptian god of wisdom
and communication. You might also know him as the Roman
god Mercury, which is the name of the enigmatic planet in our
solar system that, according to astrology, causes so much trouble
in our highly technological world when it goes into retrograde
and gives the illusion of orbiting backwards.

Let's come full circle now from the god and the planet of
communication, back to a hot summer's day when I was sitting

in my garden and I could not get 'as above, so below' out of my head. Why did it refuse to move on from my bank of thoughts? It stubbornly kept prodding my attention and would not go away for many months. I would come back to pondering its meaning over and over again.

What did this principle really mean? The ancient Egyptians evidently thought it was so important that they spent decades building pyramids to minutely align with the distant stars in what they called the Duat or abode of the dead. At that time, I was still beginning to delve deeply into what energy is all about. I had learnt that a wave of vibration travels in a particular direction and therefore has a predictable destination, like a soundwave that we pick up with our ears. Or the waves of light from a star that travel for billions of light years and are absorbed by our eyes, even when the actual star died long ago. Energy becomes physical matter and creates a physical world, but it does not lose the essence of what it represents. So there is a mirroring of the insubstantial and the corporeal. How would that show up for us in our physical world? As repeating experiences or synchronicity, I reasoned.

So synchronicity reveals the underlying pattern of energy which will become manifested in our physical world as matter. When you see recurring numbers or a name in seemingly unconnected places, you are witnessing the hidden pattern of energy that is expressing itself in your life.

Mirrored Events

Since I have been living an energy-directed life, I have constantly experienced incredible levels of synchronicity. One of the craziest recent examples concerned the artist Banksy. During the summer of 2020, various Banksy paintings were sold for astronomical amounts. One morning, I was scrolling through the headlines on my phone when I happened upon an article about a Banksy artwork in which he had updated a seascape with the addition of a couple of discarded orange lifejackets on the beach. I read the article, thought no more of it and got on with my day. That evening, I decided to relax in front of a film. As I scrolled through the endless choices, nothing appealed to me. Then my eye landed on a possible choice. It was *Ocean's 8*, starring Sandra Bullock. I decided it would perfectly suit my mood.

Now let me set up the situation for you: the film came out in 2018 and American movies don't usually tend to include much British culture as a rule. I sat down to watch *Ocean's 8* and within the first ten minutes I pressed the pause button and sat in stunned silence. I had just watched the main characters set the scene for a heist by walking into an art gallery. There, they caused confusion and distraction by art bombing the place, leaving a small painting. Someone asked, 'Is it a Banksy?' I had to do a double-take for a microsecond, as I remembered the article I had read that morning. Within less than 12 hours, two seemingly random occurrences involving Banksy had taken place in my life, defying normal space and time.

This Banksy episode was an example of a phenomenon that I have come to call 'mirrored events', which I have observed on many occasions. This is when there are two seemingly unrelated occurrences within a short space of time that contain similar aspects, and which can offer us a message if we look close enough. The message for me in the Banksy mirrored events was to remember that not all is as it seems. Both the news feature and the film featured paintings that had been altered – one with life jackets and the other by replacing sailors with women. At the time, I had a decision to make and I needed to see behind the facade of a situation as to what was really going on.

Our thoughts are waves of vibration and they are directional. Out of all of the hundreds of films, why did I choose that one without consciously knowing what it contained? Synchronicity is the hidden patterning of energy. Its presence shows up as the recurring symbols that appear in your life. Whether it is in music, numbers, names, people or signs, you are witnessing the fabric of the Universe at work. 'As above, so below.' As energetically, so physically.

Become consciously aware of the synchronicities when they show up in your life. They are indicating that there is a pattern of energy at work and that something particular will manifest in time.

Global Energy Principle 23

Never assume anything. Follow the energy instead.

H ave you heard the saying 'never ASSUME, it makes an ASS out of U and ME'. Never a truer word was said!

I'm going to start by telling you a story about assumption. I went into the bathroom and saw one of those thin-legged spiders balancing on the edge of the bathroom mirror. I watched what it did. First, it checked the new surface with two legs and then it moved onto the mirror surface. As it caught sight of its reflection, it got scared and immediately retreated. It saw a spider sitting beneath it! It made a couple more false starts and then realised that the spider that seemed to be sitting right under it, ready to eat it... wasn't there. As soon as it realised the true situation, it happily crawled across the mirror, ignoring its reflection.

It puts me in mind of how many people are brainwashed by all the false news and confusing information out there – the 'false spiders'. Always check the motivation behind others' behaviour and actions. Often, they are reflecting something that isn't really there...

The Art of Non-Assumption

A few years ago, I came to a place of clarity about an insight that turned out to be a huge discovery. That place of clarity consisted of the wonderful revelation that I know nothing about anything at all! Now, it might seem strange to you that this would be a wonderful discovery and that I came to this conclusion, but I can confirm that it was just so. I will explain why.

Beauty and simplicity or total confusion and fear exist all at the same time and in the very same moment, and either state can be experienced depending on where you are in your life. What makes the difference? The way your mind operates. Your mind needs something to feed it information, so that it can come to a conclusion about how harmless or harmful the situation you are in is for you. The majority of the information comes from your previous experiences; the way you reacted to them and what the outcome was.

So what happens if you give your mind no autobiographical information at all to work with? What happens if you show up in a situation and take the stand that you know nothing about anything at all? Your mind cannot kick-start its usual process of assuming things about the situation. What does that leave? An empty stage for you to observe what shows up. What shows up will be the most truthful version of your reality, because you are placing no judgement on it from your previous experiences.

Now you can truthfully say that you do know one thing – which is that something will show up. When it does show up, you can freely choose how you react to it. You can quickly observe if your mind starts to use its threat mechanism tools. Then you can choose to stop it or to go ahead and act in a reactive way. What that means is that you have observed that you are totally responsible and in control of the outcome of the choice you make.

I call this the art of non-assumption. One of the benefits is that you observe things that otherwise you would have missed if you let your mind only use the information of your past experiences. This gives you a huge advantage when it comes to avoiding making mistakes.

What Do You Expect to See?

Let me give you a practical example of how the art of non-assumption works.

➤ Visit my website using the link on page 8, where you will find an image of a room. Have a good look at the picture and answer this question: how many red objects can you see?

➤ This number is really important and I would like you to get a piece of paper and a pen and write down what you think the figure is. (There is a very specific question below but please do *not* read on until you have written down your answer.)

➤ Now come out of my website.

➤ Next, answer the following question: without looking at the image again, how many blue objects were in the room?

➤ Which of the following does your answer fall into?

A. You don't know because you only looked at the red objects, as you assumed only the red objects were important. You assumed I was going to ask a question about the red objects. You only observed half of what was there.

B. You looked at the picture in its entirety and noticed that there were blue objects, so you can honestly say that there is at least one blue object in the room. You know there was at least one thing. You assumed my question would be about the red objects, but you were also aware that there was more in the picture than what you were counting.

C. You counted both the red and blue objects because you did not assume that just because I asked you to count the red objects, this meant that any further questions would also be about the red objects. You didn't assume that you should ignore the blue objects. You used your awareness to notice everything that was there.

There is no right or wrong answer. The actual number of blue objects is not important. The only importance of this exercise lies in you determining what your starting point is. By discovering whether your starting point was A, B or C, you already know one thing about the situation: namely, whether you are inclined to make assumptions and then limit your powers of observation because of them.

This exercise shows that when we assume something, we immediately shut down the possibility of noticing anything outside of what we believe. The path of logical thinking then takes over. We are likely to interpret any subsequent information about the situation based on the first assumption we made. We make snap judgements about people in the first few seconds.

Sometimes we choose to ignore blatant evidence that our first assumption was wrong. Why? Because our egos cannot stand to admit that we have made a mistake. This can lead to more mistakes, until something so acute happens that we simply cannot ignore it anymore. The choice we are now faced with is often much more difficult because first we have to come out of a state of denial, admit we got it wrong and deal with the feelings of embarrassment, shame, guilt, anger and regret we may be faced with. If we can avoid all of this in the first place, we don't fall into the trap and therefore we don't have to spend time getting back on track with our lives.

When you are talking with someone or you are about to go somewhere, start by saying to yourself: 'I know nothing about anything at all.' Let go of your mind's need to be in control. Relax and you will be amazed at what you notice. It may even change your outlook completely.

Global Energy Principle 24

Become consciously aware of the impact your thoughts have on others. Even if you do not think you are acting them out, energy reveals all.

Several years ago, a film called *What the Bleep Do We Know!?* came out, which introduced me to the work of an incredible man. That man was called Dr Masaru Emoto and I had the great privilege of seeing him give a live lecture a few years later. What Dr Emoto discovered turned the world on its head.

Dr Emoto was a Doctor of Alternative Medicine in Japan; a researcher, author and entrepreneur who enquired into the energetic power of our thoughts and what they create. He knew about micro clusters and he studied the structure of water, most especially the crystals of frozen water.

The human body is made up of over 80 per cent of water and Dr Emoto wanted to know how the quality of our thoughts affected the health of the water in our bodies. He took flasks of water and experimented with directing different qualities of thoughts at them. He then froze the water and studied the structure of the water crystals which formed. What he discovered was astonishing.

What Difference a Single Thought Makes

Dr Emoto put pieces of paper with life-affirming words under his flasks of frozen water. These were the words:

➤ I love you.

➤ Thank you.

➤ I am grateful for you.

Love, forgiveness and gratitude produced the most beautiful and exquisite crystals. Beautiful, symmetrical structures giving a feeling of balance and growth. Just like a perfect snowflake.

Interestingly, Dr Emoto's choice of words echoes the simplest form of the Polynesian Ho'oponopono forgiveness prayer, which became popular in the West at the end of the last decade. That form of the prayer is:

I'm sorry.
Please forgive me.
Thank you.
I love you.

Dr Emoto also directed harsh, heartless words at the flasks of water. Words such as:

➤ You are stupid

➤ I hate you

➤ I am going to kill you

When he looked at the water crystals that had formed, he saw a destroyed and devastated mess with no definition and no symmetry. From his experiments, it was becoming evident that the water inside us morphs vibrationally to take on the shape of the quality of our thoughts. Like a chameleon that takes on the colours of its surroundings, water reflects our internal environment.

When discussing his findings, Dr Masaru Emoto talked about the concept of Hado: 'Hado is the intrinsic vibrational pattern at the atomic level in all matter, the smallest unit of energy. Its basis is the energy of human consciousness.' In Japanese, the term 'Hado' means 'wave motion or vibration' and has been known about for a long time.

Water is everywhere. Without water, hardly anything could live. This means that everywhere there is water, the quality of our thoughts and the way we live will affect the healthiness and harmony of our fluid environment. We are intrinsically interwoven with this living elixir.

Dr Emoto went on to study the effect of the collective consciousness in great bodies of water around the globe. He took samples from the tap water in London, Paris and Tokyo and found there were no crystals, just featureless blobs. He took samples of water before and after it was blessed by a priest. Where there had been no crystals, beautiful and complex forms grew that he captured in photographs. He also researched into what water looks like before and after we use a mobile phone and a microwave oven near it. The water goes from producing symmetrical, diamond-like crystals to destroyed and debased forms that bear no resemblance to them.

So the power of the feelings of love, gratitude and forgiveness is real. Consciousness has measurable effects on the structure of water crystals. The more you embody those vibrations, the more the water in your body transforms into a healthy, coherent, life-giving force. The way you treat yourself determines how healthy your energy vibrations are and affects the health of the water in the cells of your body; that vital 80 per cent of which you are made.

If You Were a 3D Printout

Since the invention of the 3D printer, our world is rapidly becoming a place in which more and more objects can be printed. Houses are printed with concrete in South America; coral reefs are printed with the polyps embedded to repopulate the reef beds. Recycled plastic is printed into new products and, in medicine, scientists are printing blood vessels and tissues, and even stem cells.

If you were a 3D printout, what would you come out as? How would your thoughts shape the mould? What would your emotional state show to the world? Imagine if we could print with light and vibration in a way that everyone could see the result. What would you look like?

While we might not be able to do that just yet, a 3D vibrational printout of you exists every day. You leave a mark on the world. Your choices, your actions, your thoughts and emotions dictate what happens to you and to those around you. Energy reveals all.

Energy is the new frontier for humankind to discover, yet it is also the ancient gateway to natural optimisation. It has been misunderstood for a long time. When we use the word 'energy', it brings to mind lightbulbs, sports drinks and electricity. Now you know that energy is so much more; in fact, it is everything. It is what forms your body, the world around you and the fabric of the Universe. Natural energy and healthy vibrations ensure that you can thrive and derive maximum benefit from the opportunities that surround you.

The man-made, non-biological frequencies which are being used more and more are disruptors of your vital life force. Becoming energy aware gives you the knowledge to ensure that you are now able to understand the laws of energy and how to harness them to live a life of no mistakes.

The 24 Energy Principles in this book will give you a groundbreaking advantage. They can stop you from making the mistakes that keep you from enjoying deeper relationships, reaching high levels of happiness and being able to do extraordinary things with your life. *Energy Aware* invites you to experience the unseen vibrational realm that is your birthright. The natural world has been successfully using this world beyond logic for billions of years; and now it is your turn...

My aim in this book has been to give you access to a way of living which dramatically cuts down the mistakes that you have been making. To help you to lower the risk of you making mistakes now and in the future. By becoming energy aware, you will gain access to an unerring route map that can keep you on track every time you have a decision to make, every day. You can now become aligned with who you truly are and what you truly need. You are now able to accomplish seemingly extraordinary things. The time has come to fully embrace the unseen vibrational world that exists within you and around you all of the time. Simply put, your future depends on it.

In the next chapter, I have created a simplified way to help you understand what is happening with your energy at any given time.

Your Battery For Life

Do you remember the Duracell Bunny? The pink rabbit that the company has used for 27 years to show how their alkaline batteries last and last? Well, the Duracell Bunny is nothing compared to the living battery that is your biofield. It is your battery for life. Let me tell you about the superior benefits of your battery:

➤ It doesn't need plugging in.

➤ It doesn't cost you any money to get one.

➤ It is available 24/7.

➤ It doesn't need renewing.

➤ It is truly everlasting while you are alive – and even beyond!

➤ It doesn't run out of storage space, which you then have to pay to increase.

And, best of all, it is your personal battery. You get it before you are born and it stays with you for your entire life. Every living being has one.

If you use it with care, your battery for life will be your best friend and help you to stay healthy and happy. However, just like any battery, it can run out of energy and end up working at a very poor level. When that happens, it is because your energy is being tied up in ways that are not serving you. When your energy is tied up, it is unavailable to you, just like a battery that only has enough power to create a dim light or which takes ages to start a car. Let's take a look next at six states in which we may find ourselves losing power.

The Six Battery States That Lose You Power

There are six main ways in which any battery can lose power. Whether you think about your mobile phone battery, a standard alkaline battery or a car battery, my aim is to give you a simple model that you can use to check in and diagnose what is happening to your own energy.

1. Used-up capacity

A battery has a certain amount of energy capacity at which it works at full power. If your mobile is using up too much storage through running an application like Facebook or is storing too many photos or videos, this can eat up the energy rapidly. When it is used up, the power drops.

Do you feel like you have taken on too much? Have you got too many irons in the fire or are you stretching yourself too thin? If you have used up too much storage on your phone, you have to identify which files you don't need and delete them. Sometimes, it is not obvious which applications are eating up your storage. And it is the same in your life: if you are saying 'yes' to those activities that are costing your battery too much energy, there will come a time when you will become depleted. If you are running on empty, with no more capacity to take on any more, you are at risk of burnout. You can experience high stress and anxiety states or crashed moods.

I have created a quick reference guide that you can check to see how much energy capacity you are likely to have and what you need to change now before you reach the low power stage.

In the section 'Energy Aware Tools', I will be sharing some tools that you can use to charge up your battery for life, once you have identified which battery state you are in.

The Traffic Lights Battery-For-Life Stress Monitor

Here is a way to check the quality of your day-to-day life and pick up on specific markers of how healthy your stress responses are. The following table lists the top three indicators for you to pay attention to:

GREEN: mild and manageable	AMBER: continuous and concerning	RED: dangerous and damaging
How to recognise the green stage:	How to recognise the amber stage:	How to recognise the red stage:
1. Occasional worrying.	1. Your stomach might often be in a tight knot and you may find it difficult to switch off and sleep. You can wake up feeling a lack of energy for the day ahead.	1. You might feel high levels of anxiety, depression or a feeling of impending doom.
2. Headaches and digestion problems often diagnosed as irritable bowel syndrome.	2. Ceaseless worrying about things that didn't bother you before.	2. You may be suffering from insomnia as you can't switch off, even though you are feeling totally exhausted. If you are waking up at 3 am, this may be because the hormone cortisol is trying to prepare you for the high stresses of the day ahead. This is the time it starts spiking. Another symptom of high stress levels is jaw clenching and grinding your teeth.
3. Irritation and mild frustration.	3. Your workload may have started to feel like a chore instead of a joy.	3. You may be confused, forgetful and have mood swings, isolating yourself from others and finding it hard to socialise.
If you recognise these symptoms then you need to find ways to relax, get enough sleep and eat properly.	It is time to find out where the stress is piling up and actively reduce those things that are high stress triggers in your life.	If you recognise the red symptoms and you don't address this dangerous and damaging condition, you are at risk of serious physical illnesses and psychological problems such as depression and chronic anxiety. You need to look seriously at your life and reduce your stress levels immediately. You could end up with adrenal fatigue, which takes a long time to recover from. Seek professional help.

The three traffic light states

2. Reversed Polarity

Imagine one of those big torches that light up your path in the dark. They need an alkaline battery to create light. The light can only be activated when a closed electric circuit is created. This happens through the connection of a positively charged cathode and a negatively charged anode; when your battery touches the terminals in the torch case and you switch the button on, you have light. However, you must connect up the right end of the battery with the right terminal; otherwise, when you switch it on nothing happens.

You can also be in a reversed state. A good indicator is when no matter how hard you try, you just don't seem to get anywhere with your plans. Things don't seem to be connecting. You keep on asking, 'Why me? Why doesn't anything ever work out for me? When is it going to be my turn?' There are several ways in which you can recognise when this happens.

➤ You keep getting your words round the wrong way; for example, saying 'north' when you mean 'south'.

➤ You feel stuck, as if you are standing in treacle.

➤ You are writing letters the wrong way round; this is so common that proof-readers have a special symbol for correcting it.

➤ Your thinking is muddled.

If you have reversed polarity, it is important to get the current of your energy flowing in the right direction again, because otherwise this will stop you from making progress. Just as the torch won't light up no matter how many times you press the on button, your battery for life will also not be able to have a flowing current.

3. Scrambled messages

If you were transferring files from your mobile phone to another device via a USB cable and you pulled out the cable before the transfer was complete, it could end up damaging or corrupting the data on your files. A corrupted file is one with scrambled code and is unreadable. It might not be possible to recover the full data.

This is similar to when you are trying to convince yourself that something is true when it isn't. You put yourself under massive pressure and are likely to suffer from conflicting emotions. It takes a huge investment of energy to keep up the state of denial. This is because, as you know, your body is wired for truth and to constantly go against it is exhausting. You end up living life at cross-purposes, at odds with yourself.

4. Leaking

If an alkaline battery is left in a device for too long and not used, it can end up leaking. A chemical called potassium chloride gets released, which can cause burns and is toxic. If you ingest it or inhale it, another toxic chemical called potassium hydroxide can make you very ill. The battery is oozing corrosive gunk. If you tried using it, it would be dead. No charge, no energy. Leakage can damage an electronic device beyond repair.

Frustration, anger, disappointment, bitterness and resentment are the most corrosive emotions we have, and they can affect the heart. These emotions can elevate your blood pressure, keep your muscles under tension and cause poor sleep. A seven-year study on 3886 patients by Harvard Medical School showed that the risk of having a heart attack is significantly higher following an outburst of anger; the more intense the outburst, the higher the risk. Just like the leaking battery, emotions such as anger eat into your life, robbing you of joy and fulfilment and maybe even your health.

5. Stagnation

If you do not use a device for a long time, it stagnates. If you don't use a battery for a long time, it will gradually lose its power. When you feel stuck and that nothing is happening, you may be experiencing a build-up of pressure. Are you unable to let go of what is not beneficial for you? This can lead to you feeling fed up of perceiving that you have been short-changed by life and that you are forever waiting and stagnating while others are living out their dreams.

One way that we can stagnate is by over-identifying with someone else and becoming a me-too. This can happen in relationships and you can be in danger of losing your independent essence and burying your own dreams and goals instead. Of course, this state can sometimes represent exactly what you want: to be a couple and act as one. However, if that is preventing you from evolving, it can eventually become claustrophobic. Dreams and goals have a habit of showing up and reminding you of their unfinished business. They can shine a light on a lack of fulfilment.

Another way of stagnating is when you are avoiding making a choice you need to make in order to move your life on. You may be making excuses and procrastinating. Energy can get backed up like water behind a dam and the pressure builds. You can end up spending your energy on denying that anything needs to be done in your life.

6. Depletion

A depleted battery is running out of charge and shows a warning sign. If you are feeling exhausted all the time, you are not charging yourself up adequately. Are you over-extending yourself and giving away energy you do not have? You need to check whether the energy you are putting out is greater than what you are charging yourself up with. Are you getting the low-charge warning sign in your life? There are three ways in which this may be happening...

There may be someone who is taking all of your energy before you can get fully charged up again. Identify if someone around you has a dominating Emotional Teddy Bear (see pages 80–85), because that person's behaviours could be continuously depleting you. Like an unidentified bill that keeps costing you money through your phone, you may be paying in life-force energy.

In a similar vein, if you are finding yourself caught up in addictive behaviour, you may be trying to keep masked anxiety at bay. Each time you give in to the urge, you are consciously or unconsciously aiming to self-tranquilise an uncomfortable, unhappy or upsetting feeling. It may be an unresolved memory or fear of things happening in the future. It often takes tremendous willpower to resist the urge of addictions. While you are focusing on that resistance, your energy is continuously ebbing away and not being given a chance to recharge.

Are you finding that you can't say no to other people's agendas? If you always put them before your own needs, then you are not giving yourself the nourishment that you require. You are charging up everyone else's battery for life and neglecting to charge up your own.

Energy Aware Quick Reference Table

When you are feeling out of sorts and you don't really know why, the table in this section will help you to identify what is happening with you. Use this table before you make any major or important decisions so that you know:

➤ what emotional baggage you need to deal with

➤ what logical limiters you need to remove

➤ whether your energy state matches the energy of your environment.

The Process

Work through the following steps and relate each stage to the information in the relevant column in the table overleaf:

➤ Ask yourself: what is my current emotional and/or mental state? For example, do I feel anxious, low, angry or confused? Identify and accept your current state.

➤ Identify what to focus on – for example, unresolved business from the past or a need to forgive.

➤ Using the table, look at the battery-for-life state to understand what is happening with your energy.

➤ Understand which vortex of light is being triggered.

➤ Go to the Energy Aware Tools section on pages 207–18 and use them to get yourself into the ideal state to feel better and be ready to make those decisions you need to make.

State of Being	Associated Vortex of Light	Battery-For-Life State	What to Focus On
Insecurity	Earth	Scrambled message	Take time to understand where your feeling of insecurity is coming from: what past experience are you still carrying the wounds of?
Anger, blame	Root	Leaking	Identify where you feel that you have lost control in your life. Do you need to forgive yourself or someone else? Go to Relationship Energy Principle 14.
Disempowerment, helplessness	Sacral	Depletion	Take time to identify which of your inner resources you do not have access to. Is it self-love, self-esteem, self-worth? Go to Personal Energy Principle 6.
Fear, anxiety	Solar Plexus	Used-up capacity	Go to Personal Energy Principle 1 and use the Survival Calculation to find out where your mind sees a threat to your physical survival.
Grief, jealousy	Heart	Leaking	Identify what you feel you have lost. Grief can come in many guises. Go to Personal Energy Principle 13.
Compassion fatigue	Universal Heart	Depletion	Be kind to yourself and go to Relationship Energy Principle 14. Refresh yourself with some energy magic. (See page 130.)

Jadedness	Transcendental Heart	Stagnation	Identify where you have given up on your dreams and goals. Go to Relationship Energy Principle 15 and dive deep into extended gratitude.
Feeling stifled	Throat	Stagnation	Have you given up your personal throne? Go to Personal Energy Principle 9.
Confusion	Third Eye	Reversed polarity	Go to Personal Energy Principle 2. Use your inner Yes/No with your name and find out if your thinking is back to front.
Hopelessness	Cosmic Third Eye	Stagnation	Identify if you are in the habit of unhappiness. Go to Relationship Energy Principle 12.
Procrastination	Crown	Stagnation	Identify what the underlying fear is about the decision you need to make.
Doubt	Halo	Used-up capacity	Identify what emotions you are feeling. Go to Global Energy Principle 22 and look for the synchronicity in your life to bring yourself back on track.
Despair	Soul Star	Leaking	Identify where you have lost your faith in life. Go to Energy Principle 8 and reconnect with your heart.

The Energy Aware quick reference table

Universal Heart Magic

Sit comfortably and focus your attention on breathing into your heart, powering up its energy. When you breathe out, send the energy into the huge toroidal field that stretches out from your heart. Keep doing this cyclic breathing to bring fresh energy into your Universal Heart vortex of light.

As mentioned, in the final chapter of this book, I will be offering you a set of Energy Aware tools. They will help you to get proactive in using your biofield as a massive resource to help yourself, and will help to set you up to be able to make Bright Choices and score a bullseye every time.

Energy Aware Tools

n this chapter, I will be sharing some powerful Energy Aware tools with you. They are designed to enable you to use your own biofield proactively as a vibrational resource; to go beyond your mind and change the frequencies of your emotions and thoughts. With these energy tools, you can alter your life a little more every day and design your life to avoid making mistakes. They will set you up for achieving the three parts of the empowered choice cycle so that you can make Bright Choices and create an extraordinary life. You can use these Energy Aware tools to be an inner activist and an outer change maker.

Changing Emotional Resonance

The way we feel in this moment seldom starts here; the root cause exists in the past. You now know about sympathetic resonance and that emotions are vibrations of energy. This Energy Aware tool is designed to help you to transmute whichever distressing emotion you are feeling now. By harnessing sympathetic resonance, use this tool to change the energy of the memory that is triggering how you feel.

➤ Begin by asking yourself: when have I felt like this in the past?

➤ Now go to Personal Energy Principle 2 and follow the instructions on using your inner Yes/No on pages 63–4. You are going to use this to feel the connection between your past emotions and what you are feeling now.

➤ Name an emotion out loud and then use your Yes/No to confirm it. You can use the following list:

  ➤ anxiety

  ➤ fear

  ➤ anger

  ➤ grief

  ➤ guilt

  ➤ disillusionment

  ➤ resentment

  ➤ regret

  ➤ betrayal

  ➤ abandonment

➤ Experiment and add your own emotions to the list.

➤ Next, I would like you to visualise two tuning forks: one inside of you and one that is placed in a sphere about a metre (or two feet) in front of you.

➤ Bring up the relevant memory and imagine it in the sphere with the tuning fork inside it.

➤ Visualise this tuning fork vibrating within the memory you have identified and see it taking on the vibration of the upsetting feeling that memory still creates within you.

➤ Assign a sound to that vibration. See and hear the whole of the sphere vibrating with it.

➤ Now imagine vibrating the same frequency of the emotion through the tuning fork in your body. Feel that you are receiving the vibration in your body from the tuning fork in the sphere in front of you until you are vibrating with the same resonance.

➤ Finally, feel the tuning fork inside your body switch to a different frequency of vibration: that of calm. Assign a sound to the vibration and fine-tune it. At the same time, visualise the tuning fork in the sphere changing to the calm vibration, until you feel a sense of calm in both the past and the present. Hear the sound of the upsetting feeling become the sound of calmness.

Create Your State

Set your biofield to resonate with a life-affirming energy state. Just as it is possible to change the pattern of a cloth that is being woven, you can decide what state you want to vibrate in. This tool helps you to make sure the resonance in your biofield matches up with what you wish to manifest during your day.

➤ Decide on what kind of state you wish to create – whether it is one of joy, peace, abundance or excitement, or any other life-affirming state. Bring to mind a time when you felt that state in the past.

➤ Use all of your five senses to immerse yourself in that memory. Spend a couple of minutes focusing on each part:

   ➤ *Visual:* your sense of sight. What vision evokes that state?

   ➤ *Auditory:* your sense of hearing. What sound evokes that state?

   ➤ *Kinaesthetic:* your sense of touch. What touches your skin to evoke that state?

   ➤ *Olfactory:* your sense of smell. What scent evokes that state?

   ➤ *Gustatory:* your sense of taste. What food or drink evokes that state?

➤ Then focus on the following:

   ➤ *Emotional:* what feeling evokes that state?

   ➤ *Mental:* what thought evokes that state?

➤ Stay in the full sensory, emotional and mental memory for at least five minutes.

➤ Now, put your hands on your heart, with your dominant hand on top, and breathe in three times. Each time, breathe the memory into your heart.

➤ Allow all of the aspects of yourself that you have evoked

to pour into the current moment and feel them flood your system.

➤ Sit with this sensualised state for a few moments and keep breathing into your heart, before consciously sending the feeling you've built up into the positive state you want to feel.

Power Statement

This is an update for affirmations, in which you create a power statement to reflect what you actually believe before you start using it. As we have seen, it is no good reciting something that you do not believe.

➤ A power statement is a statement of intention about how you want to show up in the world. When phrasing yours, be sure to include the following elements:

➤ What you are grateful for

➤ What you want to bring into your life

➤ What you want to send out to others and the world

➤ Use your inner Yes/No to check each part of your power statement, and remember that a power statement should always include the vibration of gratitude.

➤ Finish your power statement with the words: 'Let the energetic truth of this sink into my bones. For the highest good.'

➤ Write out your power statement and use it every morning after you have used the 'create your state' tool.

Energy Ball

With this tool, you proactively shape your energy and play with the invisible vibrations in your biofield.

➤ Start to visualise roots growing from the base of your spine and reaching down into the solid Earth. You are connected with the Earth, bound to the soil and perfectly grounded.

➤ Allow the Earth's energy to move up through the roots, filling every inch of your body. Gather this energy as if you are a battery charging up.

➤ When you feel like you have enough energy, hold your hands out in front of you, keeping them steady and with the palms facing each other. See an opening appear in both of your hands. A portal has been opened and the energy is flowing out.

➤ Feel the energy swirling and building up between your hands. Feel that the energy is coalescing into a ball between your hands, becoming denser and denser.

➤ Once you can feel the ball of energy between your hands, set the intention for it to become any colour that you want. Visualise that colour spreading through your energy ball until it is glowing brightly.

➤ Play with your energy ball by pushing your hands closer together or taking them further apart and notice how the energy expands to match your actions.

➤ Now that you have added a colour, try adding a sound. Hum at the pitch you are naturally drawn to make. Feel the energy intensify.

➤ Add an intention for what you would like to amplify in your life. Take a deep breath in and blow your intention into your energy ball.

➤ Pull your hands out as far as they will go from your body and step into your energy ball. Take a deep breath in and feel the vibrations align with how you want to feel.

Stir Your Crucible of Creation

Once you know how to create your energy ball, you can use it in a different way. We have a saying, 'making waves', meaning to do something that affects the course of a situation. Historically, it has been used in a negative context, but it is time to change it up to mean that we are creating a positive advantage. We know instinctively that waves create change. If you want to start a change in the world, you can use this to create the energy waves that will form the vibrational platform on which you can become an outer change maker.

➤ Activate your intention and visualise a large crucible in front of you.

➤ When you have created your energy ball (see page 212), place it into your crucible.

➤ Start stirring your ball clockwise. As you stir, imagine pulling into the moving energy all of the resources, people, opportunities and guidance you need.

➤ Now, visualise the ripples spreading out far and wide, just like the arms of a galaxy, influencing positive change in the world.

Set Yourself a Synchronicity Marker

A synchronicity marker is a sign, symbol, number or anything else that will indicate that you are successfully manifesting what you want, both internally and externally.

➤ Put the intention into your consciousness for that marker to show up in your reality whenever you are in alignment with what you want to create in your life. Remember: 'As above, so below.'

Vortices of Light Energising Workout

This tool will put your vortices of Light through a workout and raise the vibrations in your biofield. It is a vibrational power-up. (If you wish, you can add the specific musical note by visiting my website via the link on page 8 and using the Tone Generator resource until you have memorised all the notes.)

➤ **Earth vortex:** focus your attention on a point a foot below your feet. Visualise a pinpoint of turquoise and Earth-brown swirling light there. Breathe in and then, when you breathe out, visualise the light expanding. Take three slow, deep breaths and each time you exhale, visualise the ball of light growing bigger and bigger. Keep focusing your attention a foot below your feet and begin to tone a DUMM sound. Hum on the note F#. As you intone the note, make the connection with the turquoise and Earth-brown swirling ball of energy below your feet and feel it resonating with your Earth vortex. Repeat the note three times.

➤ **Root vortex:** focus your attention on the base of your spine. Visualise a pinpoint of red light there. Breathe in and then, when you breathe out, visualise the red light expanding. Take three slow, deep breaths and each time you exhale, visualise the red ball of light growing bigger and bigger. Keep focusing your attention on the base of your spine and begin to tone a UH sound. Hum on the note G. As you intone the note, make the connection with the red ball of energy at the base of your spine and feel it resonating with your root vortex. Repeat the note three times.

➤ **Sacral vortex**: focus your attention on the point just under your navel and visualise a bright orange pinpoint of light. Take a breath in and, when you breathe out, visualise the orange light expanding into a ball. Take three deep breaths and each time you exhale, visualise the ball of light expanding. Make the vowels sound OOO as if you were saying the word 'you'. Hum on the note A. Make the connection between the sound you are intoning and the orange ball of light at your navel and your sacral vortex. Repeat the sound three times.

➤ **Solar plexus vortex:** focus your attention on your stomach area. Visualise a pinpoint of bright yellow light. Take a deep breath in and, when you breathe out, breathe into the pinpoint of yellow light and visualise it expanding. Take three slow, deep breaths and each time you exhale, visualise the yellow ball of light expanding. The tone sound for the solar plexus chakra is OH. Hum on the note B. As you make the sound, feel the connection resonating with your stomach area and solar plexus vortex. Repeat the sound three times.

➤ **Heart vortex:** focus on the centre of your chest and visualise a pinpoint of bright green light there. Take a deep breath in and, when you breathe out, visualise the light expanding. Take another three deep breaths and each time you exhale, visualise the green ball of light expanding. Intone the vowel AH. Hum on the note C. Feel the connection between the sounds and the centre of your chest and your heart vortex. Repeat the tone three times.

➤ **Universal heart vortex:** take your attention to about half a metre or a foot in front of your heart vortex and visualise a pinpoint of bright pink light. Take a deep breath in and, when you exhale, visualise the light in front of you starting to expand. Take another three breaths and each time you exhale, visualise the pink light expanding in front of you into a ball of light. Intone the sound AWE just as you pronounce it. Hum on the note that feels natural to you. Feel the connection between the sound you are making and the ball of light in front of you. This resonant connection stretches out from your physical body and connects with your universal heart vortex. Repeat the sound three times

➤ **Transcendental heart vortex:** focus about a metre, or two feet, out from your heart vortex and visualise a pinpoint of bright silver light. Take a deep breath in and, when you exhale, visualise the silver light expanding in front of you. Take another three breaths and each time you exhale, see the silver light expanding to form a ball of silver light. Tone the sound YAY and feel the connection between your physical body and the point two feet in front of you. Hum on a note that feels natural to you. Feel the resonant relationship. Repeat the sound three times.

➤ **Throat vortex:** focus your attention on your throat and visualise a pinpoint of bright blue light there. Take a deep breath in and, when you breathe out, visualise the blue light expanding at your throat. Take another three breaths and each time you exhale, visualise the light expanding. The sound for this chakra is EYE. Hum on the note D. As you make the sound, feel it resonating in your throat, making the connection between the sound and the energy in your throat vortex. Repeat the sound three times.

➤ **Third eye vortex:** visualise a pinpoint of deep blue light between your eyebrows. Take a deep breath in and, as you breathe out, visualise that point of light expanding. Take another three breaths and each time you exhale, visualise the deep blue light expanding more and more. Tone the sound AYE and hum on the note E. Feel the resonant connection with the point of your third eye vortex between your brows. Repeat the tone three times.

➤ **Cosmic third eye vortex:** focus about half a metre or a foot in front of your third eye vortex and visualise a pinpoint of pale lavender light. Take a deep breath in and visualise the light expanding when you exhale. Take three more slow breaths and each time you exhale, see the light expanding more and more. Tone the sound HOO and hum on a note that feels natural to you. Feel the connection between your head and the point in front of you. Feel the resonant relationship. Repeat the sound three times.

➤ **Crown vortex:** focus your attention on the top of your head and visualise a pinpoint of bright violet light. Take a deep breath in and, when you breathe out, visualise the lights expanding. Take another three breaths and each time

216

you exhale, visualise the violet light expanding more and more. Make the sound EEE and hum on the note F. Feel the sound resonating in the top of your head and with your crown vortex. Repeat the sound three times.

➤ **Halo vortex:** focus a foot above your head and visualise a pinpoint of golden light. Take a deep breath in and visualise the light expanding when you exhale. Take three more slow breaths and, each time you exhale, see the light expanding more and more. Tone the sound AAA and hum on a note that feels natural to you. Feel the connection between your head and the point, about half a metre or a foot above you, of your halo vortex. Feel the resonant relationship. Repeat the sound three times.

➤ **Soul star vortex:** visualise a pinpoint of brilliant white light about a metre or two feet above your head. Take a deep breath in and, as you breathe out, visualise that point of light expanding. Take another three breaths and each time you exhale, visualise the bright white light expanding more and more. Intone the sound TING and hum on a note that feels natural to you. Feel the resonant connection between your whole body and your soul star vortex above your head. Repeat the tone three times.

Extra Energy Aware Tools from this Book

Ho'oponopono

If you feel you need to let go of a grudge, use the Polynesian Ho-oponopono forgiveness prayer. You can use my version in Relationship Energy Principle 14 or any other version that you resonate with. Or write your own version.

RAAK

To amplify the power of your heart field, get into the habit of using RAAK or random acts of anonymous kindness. Go back to Relationship Energy Principle 14 to remind yourself of how to use this Energy Aware tool.

Bibliography

The Wise Child Inside You

Daniel, R. (2017). 'ElectroBee ERC'. DOI: https://research-information.bris.ac.uk/en/projects/electrobee-erc

SciFi (2014). 'Shake your silk-maker' [online video]. Available at: youtube.com/watch?v=mq-r20mlGes

Part One: The Vibrational Human

Becker, R. (1999). *Cross Currents*. New York: Penguin Group (USA) Inc.

Chang, J., Fisch, J., Popp, A. (1998). *Biophotons*. New York: Springer.

Korotkov, K. (2014). *Energy Fields: Electrophotonic analysis in humans and nature*. Russia: DrK.

Lyons, L. (2006). 'Why Do Cats Purr?'. In: *Scientific American*. Available at: scientificamerican.com/article/why-do-cats-purr (Accessed: 26 February 2021.)

Personal Energy Principle 2

Backster, C. (2003). *Primary Perception*. Anza CA: White Rose Millennium Press.

Personal Energy Principle 3

Leport, A., Stark, S., Mcgaugh, J. et al. (2016). 'Highly superior autobiographical memory'. Available at: researchgate.net/publication/298731581_A_cognitive_assessment_of_highly_superior_autobiographical_memory. DOI: 10.1080/09658211.2016.1160126

Personal Energy Principle 4

Kindersley, D. (2020). *The Physics Book*. London: Penguin Random House.

Personal Energy Principle 8

Perkins, J. (1997). *Shapeshifting*. Rochester, Vermont: Destiny Books.

Personal Energy Principle 10

Goswami, A. (2001). *Physics of the Soul*. Charlottesville, VA: Hampton Roads Publishing Company Inc.
Morehouse, D. (2008). *Remote Viewing*. Boulder, CO: Sounds True Inc.

Part Two: What Lies Between Us

McTaggart, L. (2001). *The Field*. London: HarperCollins Publishers.
Sheldrake, R. (2001). 'Experiments of the sense of being stared at'. In: *Journal of the Society for Psychical Research*, Vol. 65, pp.122–37. Available at: sheldrake.org

Relationship Energy Principle 12

S1mOne (2002). Directed by A. Niccol (film). New Line Cinema.
Mosher, C. (2014). 'How to grow stronger without lifting weights'. In: *Scientific American*. Available at: scientificamerican.com/article/how-to-grow-stronger-without-lifting-weights (Accessed: 23 December 2014.)

Relationship Energy Principle 14

Bergland C. (2012). 'Mindfulness training and the compassionate brain'. In: *Psychology Today*. Available at: psychologytoday.com/us/blog/the-athletes-way/201212/mindfulness-training-and-the-compassionate-brain (Accessed: 18 December 2012.)

Relationship Energy Principle 16

Global Oneness Project (2007). 'Sawubona' [online video]. Available at: youtube.com/watch?v=2IjUkVZRPK8

Dr Thais (2014). 'An Entire Town Reveals the Most Emotional Surprise to a Hearing-Impaired Resident' [online video]. Available at: youtube.com/watch?v=Kjep4G2OWzc

Relationship Energy Principle 19

Gurko, I. (2020). 'Suppressed Consciousness Science: Three Experiments That Change Everything'. In: *Stillness in the Storm*. Available at: https://stillnessinthestorm. com/2020/02/suppressed-consciousness-science-three-experiments-that-change-everything/ (Accessed: 20 February 2020.)

Shroder, T. (1999). *Old Souls*. New York: Simon & Schuster Paperbacks.

Part Three: Planetary Currents

Becker, R. (2018). 'Why this volcano in Ecuador sounds like it's breathing'. Available at: theverge.com/2018/6/13/17460774/ volcano-ecuador-cotopaxi-breathing-pipe-organ-asmr-infra-sound (Accessed: 13 June 2018.)

Burrell, L. (2019). *EMF Practical Guide*. France: ElectricSense.

Dent, J. (2020). 'Dental Plaque Removal by Ultrasonic Toothbrushes'. In: *MDPI*. Available at: mdpi.com/2304-6767/8/1/28/htm (Accessed: 23 March 2020.)

Fox, A. (2020). 'Wombats and Tasmanian Devils Glow Under Ultraviolet Light'. In: *Smithsonian Magazine*. Available at: smithsonianmag.com/smart-news/wombats-and-tasmanian-devils-added-list-mammals-uv-glow-180976620 (Accessed: 28 December 2020.)

Fu, J. (2010). *Yellow Emperor's Book of Internal Medicine*. China: China Renmin University Press.

Global Coherence Research (no date). 'The Science of Interconnectivity'. HeartMath Institute. Available at: heartmath.org/gci/research/global-coherence

Gurko, I. (2020). 'Suppressed Consciousness Science: Three

Experiments That Change Everything'. In: *Stillness in the Storm*. Available at: https://stillnessinthestorm. com/2020/02/suppressed-consciousness-science-three-experiments-that-change-everything/ (Accessed: 20 February 2020.)

IARC Publications. (2011). Available at: https://iarc.who.int/

Nace, T. (2018). 'We Finally Know How Birds Can See Earth's Magnetic Field'. In: *Forbes* magazine. Available at:

forbes.com/sites/trevornace/2018/04/04/we-finally-know-how-birds-can-see-earths-magnetic-field/?sh=154c62c420e1 (Accessed: 4 April 2018.)

Pineault, N. (2017). *The Non-Tinfoil Guide to EMFs*. CreateSpace.

Price, C., Williams, E., Elhalel, G. et al. (2020). 'Natural ELF fields in the atmosphere and in living organisms'. In: *Int. J. Biometeorol.*, 65, pp.85–92 (2021). https://doi.org/10.1007/s00484-020-01864-6 (Accessed: 8 February 2020.)

Shroder, T. (1999). *Old Souls*. New York: Simon & Schuster Paperbacks.

US National Weather Service: https://www.weather.gov/safety/lightning-power

Global Energy Principle 20

Yuga (2019). 'Yuga Explained'. Yuga. Available at: yuga.com/consciousness/yuga-explained (Accessed: 18 June 2019.)

Global Energy Principle 21

The Music Guild (2011). 'Cymatics of Solfeggio Frequencies in Drop of Water'. [online video] Available at: youtube.com/watch?v=QQ_zI-5Cm64&t=210s

Global Energy Principle 24

Masaru, E. (2005). *A víz rejtett bölcsessége*. Budapest: Édesvíz Kiadó.

Acknowledgements

Energy Aware was born during a turbulent and chaotic time – at the cusp of the change from the end of one era and the beginning of the next. I had to wait seven years before the time felt right to write it. I made a Bright Choice for my book and stepped into my own empowered choice cycle. At the beginning of the pandemic, when I couldn't go anywhere, I said 'Yes' to enrolling on an online writer's course. It turned out to be the most aligned decision I could possibly make. Michael Heppell is the man who created the course and the subsequent opportunity. It became a crucible of creation at an unprecedented time, a coming together of a group of amazing people on their own writing journeys. We formed the kind of strong bonds that only happen in special times. I would like to thank you, Michael, for your vision, support, your cheerfulness and enthusiasm. Thank you for believing in *Energy Aware* right from the start. You have been my inspiration for getting this book done. Thank you to the Write That Book course writers, especially my group, the brilliant #virtualcakers. I could share my ideas with you and know that I would get your total support, suggestions, encouragement and help. Sophie Johnson, Kevin Walsh, Joanne Parker, Libby Andrews and especially Steve Watson, you are all awesome. Steve, thank you for your friendship, your mentoring and weekly guidance.

I would like to thank my publisher Sue Richardson for seeing the potential in *Energy Aware* from the start and offering me the chance to mould it into a proper book. Thank you to Sue Lascelles, my brilliant editor whose careful and meticulous work gave me the final confidence to share what I have written with the world. Thank you to everyone at The Right Book Company who worked on *Energy Aware*.

A special thank you goes to a group of the best friends I

could ever have. It is extraordinary how close I have become to you when we have never met. Energy connects us at a deep level. Nancy Mueller, you have championed me every step of the way. Thank you for being a sounding board for my ideas, a great friend, a generous promoter of my work and for being a wonderful human being. Julie Saillant, I feel that you are the sister I never had. Thank you for your deep insights, your bright light and the sassy attitude which we share. You are always there to support me and to talk about the esoteric and metaphysical topics that are so important to me to discuss. Jodi Powell, you are my soul sister through ancient pathways. Thank you for teaching me about Polynesian healing and for the great and fascinating insights into how to read the world with different eyes. Thank you for your wisdom and wonderful friendship. I would like to thank my yoga teacher and dear friend Dayla Bull for the numerous beach walks and pub conversations and also for giving me constructive feedback on my writing.

I want to thank all of my clients over the years who have allowed me the opportunity to learn about how to harness and maximise our energy; and my cat Tivvy, who is my greatest guru in teaching me about energy.

Thank you to my parents Margot and Szabolcs for your support, love and encouragement. Thanks Mum for being the first person to read through *Energy Aware* and for being such a positive influence on my life and ultimately on my writing.

For information on how to book Ildiko for Masterclasses, private Life Retuning session and talks see

www.liferetuning.com

By being a reader of *Energy Aware* you have access to a further Book Bonus by going to

To contact Ildiko directly email her at **ildiko@liferetuning.com**